# Patterns and Sources of NAVAJO WEAVING

PUBLISHED BY
HARMSEN PUBLISHING COMPANY
3131 EAST ALAMEDA AVENUE, SUITE 2001
DENVER, COLORADO 80209

EDITOR: W. D. HARMSEN
EXHIBIT CURATOR: JOE BEN WHEAT
PHOTOGRAPHY: F. C. HILKER
PRINTING: TEWELL'S PRINTING AND LITHOGRAPHING COMPANY

THIRD PRINTING, 1978

©COPYRIGHT 1977 BY HARMSEN'S WESTERN AMERICANA COLLECTION

ALL RUGS SHOWN AND LISTED IN THIS CATALOGUE ARE FROM THE HARMSEN WESTERN AMERICANA COLLECTION.

LIBRARY OF CONGRESS CATALOG CARD NUMBER LC78-68721

ALL RIGHTS RESERVED — PRINTED IN THE UNITED STATES OF AMERICA

# Table of Contents

| | PAGE NO. |
|---|---|
| FOREWORD | 4 |
|    Joseph Stacey | |
| INTRODUCTION | 6 |
|    W. D. Harmsen | |
| NATIVE AMERICAN TAPESTRIES OF THE NAVAJO | 10 |
|    Carl Schaefer Dentzel | |
| PATTERNS AND SOURCES OF NAVAJO WEAVING | 11 |
|    Joe Ben Wheat | |
| RUG WEAVING REGIONS OF THE SOUTHWEST COLOR MAP | 12–13 |
| THE MODERN NAVAJO WEAVER | 15 |
|    Martin Link | |
| THE OTHER WEAVERS OF THE SOUTHWEST | 18 |
|    Richard G. Conn | |
| TECHNIQUE, TRADITION, AND TRADE | 21 |
|    Frederick J. Dockstader | |
| THE EARLY PERIOD | 29 |
| BOSQUE REDONDO AND AFTER | 32 |
| PAN RESERVATION RUG STYLES | 34 |
| GERMANTOWN BLANKETS | 37 |
| GANADO AREA | 40 |
| KLAGETOH | 43 |
| TWO GRAY HILLS | 45 |
| CRYSTAL | 48 |
| WESTERN RESERVATION | 51 |
| PUEBLO WEAVING | 52 |
| SAND-PAINTING, YEIS, AND YEIBECHAIS | 54 |
| TEEC NOS POS | 58 |
| WIDE RUINS | 61 |
| NAVAJO TWILLS | 61 |
| PICTORIAL RUGS | 64 |
| NOVELTY WEAVES OF THE NAVAJO | 67 |

PAGES 8-9 COURTESY OF ARIZONA HIGHWAYS.

# Index

| Rug Number | Description and Photo | Page |
|---|---|---|
| 1 | Early Period | 29 |
| 2 | Early Period | 30 |
| 3 | Early Period | 30 |
| 4 | Early Period | 30 |
| 5 | Early Period | 30 |
| 6 | Early Period (not illustrated) | 31 |
| 7 | Early Period | 30,31 |
| 8 | Early Period | 31 |
| 9 | Early Period | 31 |
| 10 | Early Period | 31 |
| 11 | Early Period | 31 |
| 12 | Bosque Redondo and After | 32 |
| 13 | Bosque Redondo and After | 32 |
| 14 | Bosque Redondo and After (not illustrated) | 32 |
| 15 | Bosque Redondo and After | 33 |
| 16 | Wedge Weave | 26 |
| 17 | Wedge Weave | 27 |
| 18 | Pan-Reservation Rug Style | 34 |
| 19 | Pan-Reservation Rug Style | 34 |
| 20 | Pan-Reservation Rug Styles | 34 |
| 21 | Pan-Reservation Rug Styles | 34 |
| 22 | Pan-Reservation Rug Style | 34 |
| 23 | Pan-Reservation Rug Style | 35 |
| 24 | Pan-Reservation Rug Style | 35 |
| 25 | Pan-Reservation Rug Style | 35 |
| 26 | Pan-Reservation Rug Style | 35 |
| 27 | Pan-Reservation Rug Style | 35 |
| 28 | Pan-Reservation Rug Style | 35 |
| 29 | Pan-Reservation Rug Style | 36 |
| 30 | Diyugi wearing Blanket | 27 |
| 31 | Germantown Blankets | 37,39 |
| 32 | Germantown Blankets | 37 |
| 33 | Germantown Table Runner | 37 |
| 34 | Germantown Pictorial | 38 |
| 35 | Ganado Area | 40 |
| 36 | Ganado Area | 40 |
| 37 | Ganado Area | 40 |
| 38 | Ganado Area | 41 |
| 39 | Ganado Area | 42 |
| 40 | Ganado Area | 42 |
| 41 | Ganado Area | 42 |
| 42 | Ganado Area | 42 |
| 43 | Ganado Area | 42 |
| 44 | Ganado Area | 42 |
| 45 | Klagetoh | 43 |
| 46 | Klagetoh | 44 |
| 47 | Klagetoh | 44 |
| 48 | Klagetoh | 44 |
| 49 | Klagetoh | 44 |
| 50 | Two Gray Hills | 45 |
| 51 | Two Gray Hills | 45 |
| 52 | Two Gray Hills | 46-47 |
| 53 | Crystal | 48-49 |
| 54 | Crystal | 48-49 |
| 55 | Crystal | 48-49 |
| 56 | Crystal | 48-49 |
| 57 | Crystal | 48 |
| 58 | Crystal | 48-49 |
| 59 | Crystal | 48-49 |
| 60 | Crystal (not illustrated) | 48 |
| 61 | Crystal | 50 |
| 62 | Western Reservation | 51 |
| 63 | Western Reservation | 51 |
| 64 | Western Reservation | 51 |
| 65 | Pueblo Weaving | 52 |
| 66 | Pueblo Weaving (not illustrated) | 52 |
| 67 | Pueblo Weaving | 52 |
| 68 | Pueblo Weaving | 52 |
| 69 | Pueblo Weaving (not illustrated) | 52 |
| 70 | Pueblo Weaving | 53 |
| 71 | Yei Rug (illustrated on pages 16-17) | 54 |
| 72 | Sand-Painting, Yeis, and Yeibechais (illustrated on pages 8-9) | 54 |
| 73 | Sand-Painting, Yeis, and Yeibechais | 54 |
| 74 | Sand-Painting, Yeis, and Yeibechais | 54 |
| 75 | Sand-Painting, Yeis, and Yeibechais | 54 |
| 76 | Sand-Painting, Yeis, and Yeibechais | 54 |
| 77 | Sand-Painting, Yeis, and Yeibechais | 54 |
| 78 | Sand-Painting, Yeis, and Yeibechais | 55 |
| 79 | Sand-Painting, Yeis, and Yeibechais | 55 |
| 80 | Sand-Painting, Yeis, and Yeibechais | 55 |
| 81 | Sand-Painting, Yeis, and Yeibechais | 56 |
| 82 | Sand-Painting, Yeis, and Yeibechais | 57 |
| 83 | Sand-Painting, Yeis, and Yeibechais | 57 |
| 84 | Teec Nos Pos | 58 |
| 85 | Teec Nos Pos | 58 |
| 86 | Teec Nos Pos | 58 |
| 87 | Teec Nos Pos (not illustrated) | 58 |
| 88 | Teec Nos Pos | 58 |
| 89 | Teec Nos Pos | 58 |
| 90 | Teec Nos Pos | 59 |
| 91 | Teec Nos Pos | 60 |
| 92 | Wide Ruins | 61 |
| 93 | Navajo Twills | 61 |
| 94 | Novelty Weave of Navajo | 62 |
| 95 | Novelty Weave of Navajo | 62 |
| 96 | Pictorial Rugs | 64 |
| 97 | Pictorial Rugs | 64-65 |
| 98 | Pictorial Rugs | 68 |
| 99 | Pictorial Rugs | 64-65 |
| 100 | Pictorial Rugs | 66 |
| 101 | Pictorial Rugs | 66 |
| 102 | Novelty Weaves of Navajo | 67 |
| 103 | Novelty Weaves of Navajo (not illustrated) | 67 |
| 104 | Novelty Weaves of Navajo (not illustrated) | 67 |
| 105 | Novelty Weaves of Navajo | 67 |

## Foreword

Joseph Stacey
Editor
Arizona Highways Magazine

In terms of numbers and quality this is an important exhibition, a comprehensive selection from a major collection, a tribute to the discernment of the sponsors, the excellence of the collection formed by the William D. Harmsens, and a testimonial to the industry and the artistic endeavors of our Native American weavers.

It is difficult to classify or categorize the Harmsen Collection of Western Americana. This exceptional collection reflects the private enterprise of two individuals: William D. and Dorothy Harmsen, who in little more than a quarter century have amassed a treasure of rare examples of early Americana. It would take a major museum, with added wings to display the entire Harmsen collection with emphasis on the paintings and sculptures representing several hundred great and near great artists.

Although the significance and quality of their collection is of museum standards, it is first of all a private collection reflecting the esthetic preferences, enthusiasm and, at times, the whims and caprices of the collectors.

Compared to many collectors, the Harmsens and their collection are young. Nevertheless, their point of prestige and importance has been accelerated by their meticulous dedication to authoritative researching, cataloging and documenting a valuable record of almost every inventoried piece. In the development of the Americana Collection they have sought advice and knowledge of specialists, such as Joe Ben Wheat, Curator of Anthropology, Professor, University of Colorado at Boulder. Dr. Wheat's resume includes the credits: B.A. University of California, 1937; M.S. University of Arizona, 1949 and Ph.D. University of Arizona 1953. His world wide archaeological field work is topped by a full year's research in more than 50 museums of the United States and western Europe with special interest in textiles. Upon the Harmsen's recommendation, Arizona Highways engaged Dr. Wheat to write the feature article for the magazine's important July 1974 special edition devoted exclusively to Native Southwestern Weaving. Rugs from the Harmsen collection were reproduced in full color with a spectacular Yei classic forming the wraparound cover.

The Harmsen Collection is perpetually "in action" at their town and ranch residences and at the Harmsen's Jolly Rancher offices and plants. More than one-third of the total collection is always "on loan" to Universities, Civic agencies and public and private institutions where it becomes in every sense a public asset.

Unlike most museum curators and private collectors, the Harmsens do not choose to hide their prized and valuable acquisitions in the protective obscurity of vaults and underground depositories. Theirs is the greater pleasure, the reward of sharing a deep felt love, interest and cultural participation with all Americans. Thus this comprehensive exhibition of our Indian weavers' art reaches a new audience and another level of appreciation.

PHOTO BY MARTIN LINK

# Introduction

W. D. Harmsen
Harmsen's Western Americana
Collection

At last the American Indians have become recognized as leaders and experts on native arts and crafts. Their bead and quill work, basket making, silversmithing, pottery, painting, and weaving have and are being sought by astute collectors all over the world.

The Navajo woman is not only a gifted artisan, but a source of complete and hard working craftsmanship. She raises and tends her flock, shears the sheep, cleans, combs, cards, and dyes the wool, before weaving it into useful and beautiful rugs, blankets, and tapestry. It is hoped this book will add to the dignity and artistic appreciation of these talented people.

For their invaluable work and efforts in helping to prepare this catalog, I wish to thank the following people:

Joe Stacey, for his Foreword. As editor of ARIZONA HIGHWAYS Magazine, he has done more to create interest in Indian artifacts, such as rugs, beadwork, pottery, baskets, and jewelry, than anyone in this field. His association with ARIZONA HIGHWAYS began in 1965, and he assumed full editorship in 1971. The ensuing years were the most successful in the history of the magazine, culminating in the widely acclaimed "Indian Arts and Crafts Collectors" series in 1974-1975. Joe Stacey is generally acknowledged to have strongly influenced the course of the arts, crafts, and business of Indian jewelry and related crafts. He is co-author of "Skystone and Silver," the authoritative collectors' source book on Southwest Indian jewelry.

Dr. Joe Ben Wheat, Curator of Anthropology, University of Colorado Museum, who has documented each weaving and explained each classification as to the area from which it came. His article on the three main sources — covering the history of the Pueblos, through the Spanish colonists and their influence of Saltillo weaving, to the creative genius of the Navajos — is most complete. He also was kind enough to lend his assistance as narrator of the movie, "Navajo Weaving — Patterns and Sources." Dr. Wheat is renowned for his world-wide archaeological field work and research in textiles. He holds a B.A. degree from the University of California, and received his M.S. and Ph.D. degrees from the University of Arizona.

Richard G. Conn, Curator, Department of Native Art, Denver Art Museum. His article on "The Other Weavers of the Southwest" opens a whole new field of information and takes us back to pre-historic times. His special interests are the arts and culture of western native America. He received a Masters degree in Anthropology from the University of Washington in Seattle and has been associated with the Eastern Washington Historical Society in Spokane, and the Manitoba Museum in Winnepeg, Canada. He is a member of the American Association of Museums, the Society for Historical Archaeology, and the Colorado-Wyoming Museum Association.

Dr. Carl S. Dentzel, Director of the Southwest Museum, Los Angeles, California, whose article, "Native American Tapestries of the Navajo," traces the history of weaving by the Navajo Indians. He is an authority on the cultures of aboriginal America and the European colonial civilizations, and his writings have appeared in scores of publications dealing with the history of Mexico, Central America, the United States, and the Pacific area. His research has taken him to all parts of the world, attending the Universities of Berlin, Paris, Munich, and Mexico. He is president of the Cultural Heritage Board of the City of Los Angeles, a member of the California Heritage Preservation Commission, and a representative on the Commission of the Californias.

Martin Link, Director of the Navajo Tribal Museum, Window Rock, Arizona, for his informative article on the Navajo weavers of the Four Corners region and for his assistance in furnishing information and pictures for the movie, "Navajo Weaving — Patterns and Sources." His understanding knowledge of the present-day Navajo weaver brings us up to date on the continuing craftsmanship of this proud people. His authority is established by the following credits: Member of the Board of Regents, New Mexico Archaeological Society; Board Member, Plateau Sciences Society of the Four Corners Area; Member of The Arizona Academy of Sciences; and, Past President, Arizona Museums Association.

Dr. Frederick J. Dockstader, researcher and writer in the field of Native American culture and art, and former director of the Museum of the American Indian, Heye Foundation, New York, New York. His article, "Technique, Tradition and Trade", gives needed background on the history and process of the weaving technology itself as practiced among Southwestern Indians, and the influence which changing styles and taste have had on design. The article also comments on the nature of the current market for Navajo textiles and the craft's continuing vitality. Living much of his early life on Navajo and Hopi reservations, he received his Ph.D. from Western Reserve University, and has served as a Commissioner of the Indian Arts and Crafts Board of the Interior Department. He is a Fellow at the Cranbrook Institute of Science, the American Anthropological Association, and the American Association for the Advancement of Science.

# Native American Tapestries of the Navajo

Carl Schaefer Dentzel, Director
Southwest Museum

Five hundred years ago the then known world was without cotton. Until the discovery of America textiles were made with many different kinds of materials. Europe and Africa were flax and wool continents. Asia utilized wool and of course silk. Garments and other materials were also made from other fibers but cotton was unknown.

The prehistoric peoples of the New World clothes themselves in animal skins or in cloth made and woven from the bark of trees as well as from the wool of the wild mountain sheep, or of the llama and alpaca which they raised.

In North America cotton was grown by the aboriginal people and from it they wove all kinds of wearing apparel. The renowned Indian civilizations of the American Southwest, Mexico and Central America produced superb garments, blankets, decorative arts and other materials woven from native cotton.

In South America the natives of the West Coast wove some of the finest textiles from llama and alpaca wool. Their work takes its rightful place among the world's greatest productions of art from the loom.

In the American Southwest, in prehistoric times, the Pueblo Indians in the valley of the Rio Grande of New Mexico and of the mesas of Arizona planted and irrigated cotton fields. For hundreds of years before the coming of the Spanish they wove and made superb useful things from cotton.

When the Navajo Indian people migrated into the Southwest they learned weaving from the agricultural Pueblo Indians. They became outstanding weavers and by the time the Spanish introduced sheep and other domesticated animals they soon became masters of the craft.

In the areas they occupied in what is now New Mexico and Arizona they became herdsmen. They adapted their pastoral way of life to the raising of sheep. Their flocks wandered throughout what is today known as the Navajo country.

Garments were woven as were blankets, rugs, sashes, bridles and hangings. They became masters of dyeing the wool, using coachineal and indigo. They utilized traditional designs and colors, creating textile styles that were new and different in the development of weaving in the American Southwest.

By the turn of the 20th Century Navajo weaving had become so famous throughout the United States that collectors and museums sought examples for their collections. Tourists bought the more commercial pieces but the finer works were sought by the connoisseurs of weaving. Thus the Navajo Indians created what might be called one of the first native tapestries in the United States.

Charles Avery Amsden, Curator of the Southwest Museum for many years, was the recognized authority on Navajo weaving. His masterful work entitled "Navaho Weaving: Its Technic and Its History," is the great authority on the subject. It was originally published in 1934 and has been reprinted and acclaimed ever since.

The Navajo shepherds and their flocks of sheep have had many vicissitudes throughout the years, as have had the Navajo weavers. Many great examples of their weaving left the Navajo reservation. Economic, social and political problems plagued the Navajo people. Throughout the struggles for survival they retained their great character and philosophy and continued to practice their many skills, particularly in jewelry making, blanket and rug weaving.

Now a new generation of alert, hard working, intelligent Navajo people are developing their vast reservation, studying their ancient customs, preserving their traditional arts. They deserve the understanding and cooperation of all for they have set great goals for their people.

Today as never before Navajo weaving is being appreciated and sought after by everyone interested in textile art. There is a renaissance of weaving on the Navajo reservation. Skilled artisans and artists are creating textiles of great beauty and significance. This ancient art which was almost lost now enjoys a healthy, inspiring revival. These magnificent woven creations with their superb colors, fascinating designs and enchanting presence, are indeed worthy of the designation unique Native American Tapestries.

# Patterns and Sources of Navajo Weaving

Joe Ben Wheat
Curator of Anthropology
University of Colorado
Museum

Navajo traditional weaving had three main sources—Pueblo Indian, Spanish colonists, and most important of all, the Navajo's own rich and fertile sense of design.

The Pueblo Indians had been weavers of native cotton since prehistoric times. When the Spanish explorers "discovered" Arizona and New Mexico in 1540, they were impressed by the painted and embroidered garments of the Pueblos. The women wore cotton dresses. The men wore shirts and breech cloths of cotton. In cold weather, both wore shawls or *Mantas* woven so that they were wider than long, the length being set by the fixed foundation or warp yarns, and the width by the free-moving weft yarns.

In 1598 the Spanish brought sheep and goats to serve the weaving needs of their permanent settlement in the Rio Grande Valley. These animals changed the Indians' life, for before long the Pueblos were spinning and weaving wool as they had cotton. Now the dress and manta were often of dark brown wool, or, because the long-fleeced Spanish churro sheep came in white and brown, of narrow alternating stripes of these colors.

The Spanish wove long blankets, often two identical halves sewn together. Most of their blankets were in tapestry weave, in which the wefts completely concealed the warps. Most of these were striped like the Pueblo mantas, but they introduced indigo dye and so had blue, as well as brown or black, and white.

The Navajo came late to the Southwest, before the Spanish but long after the Pueblos. Unlike most of their Apache kin, there were farmers, "Navajo" meaning "great fields." They were also acquisitive, adopting Pueblo people into their tribe, extending their boundaries, and learning new skills. At first, the Navajo wove only fine baskets with stepped triangles and zigzags for design, but after 1650 they borrowed the Pueblo upright loom and soon wove Pueblolike mantas and dresses. Basket-weaving was woman's work, and the loom became the woman's occupation. From the Spanish, whose herds they raided, they acquired their own sheep and soon made long Spanish style blankets or sarapes in tapestry, all in solid color or in the prevailing mode in stripes.

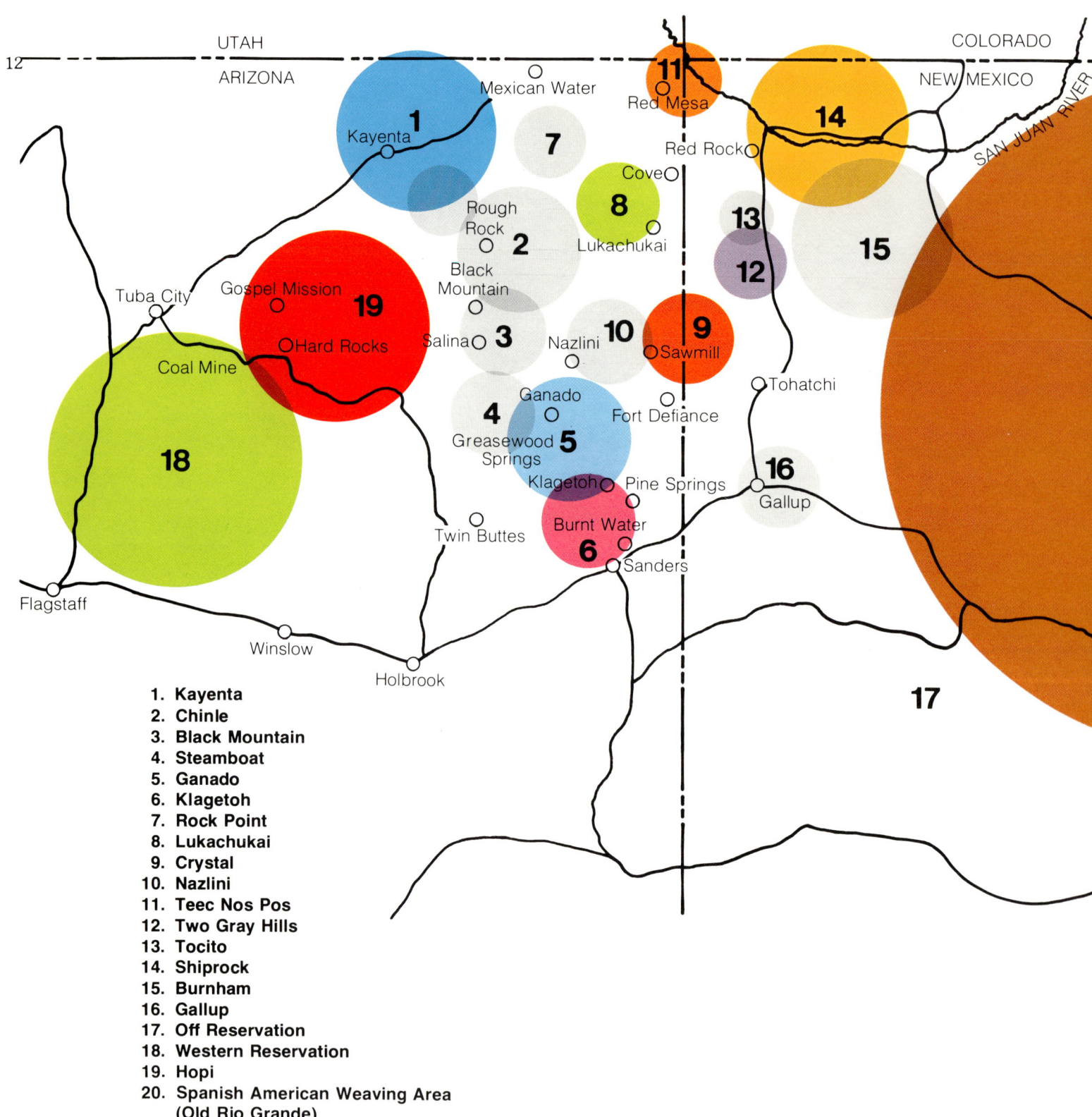

1. Kayenta
2. Chinle
3. Black Mountain
4. Steamboat
5. Ganado
6. Klagetoh
7. Rock Point
8. Lukachukai
9. Crystal
10. Nazlini
11. Teec Nos Pos
12. Two Gray Hills
13. Tocito
14. Shiprock
15. Burnham
16. Gallup
17. Off Reservation
18. Western Reservation
19. Hopi
20. Spanish American Weaving Area
    (Old Rio Grande)

**Rug weaving regions of the Southwest**
Areas color coded on the map are represented in the Harmsen exhibit.

The Spanish were temporarily driven from New Mexico by the Pueblo Revolt of 1680, but they soon returned to stay. After this, Pueblo weaving began to stagnate, as did that of the Spanish. In contrast, Navajo weaving was in its ascendency. By 1800, Navajo weaving was the most valuable product of New Mexico. They had learned to cluster simple stripes into zones or panels, and added the stepped triangles and zigzag designs from their basketry to supplement the stripes. Fine crimson wool cloth, called Bayeta, was raveled and the Navajos rewove the fine threads into their own blankets, creating bold, rich, and dignified tapestry masterpieces in dark blue, black, and white, on a rich crimson ground.

The Spanish resented the economic impact of the Navajo weavers, and to recapture some of the market, they brought two Spanish master-weavers, the Bazan brothers, to Santa Fe in 1807, to help them upgrade their weaving. With them, the Bazan brothers brought knowledge of the superb Saltillo Mexican sarapes with intricately figured and subtly colored nested diamond figures centered on a background of vertically oriented stripes of sharp-angled zigzags and tiny diamonds surrounded by a figured border. But the Spanish of the Rio Grande Valley could not match the fine Mexican colors, wools, and spinning of Saltillo. The result was a coarsened and simplified version of the Saltillo, with the figures often merged into stripes in the early tradition.

When Mexico won independence from Spain in 1821, she threw open her borders with the United States. The Santa Fe Trail commerce, which began that year as a trickle, became a flood. Costly cloth from Mexico was supplanted by cheaper cloth transported across the Plains. During this time, the Navajo increased their raiding along the Rio Grande and even into Mexico. After the Mexican war in 1846, when New Mexico and Arizona became a part of the United States, the Navajo continued their raiding against Mexicans and Americans alike. All this came to an abrupt end in 1863. Kit Carson defeated the Navajo, in part by destroying their sheep. Humbled, the once fierce Navajo were moved to Bosque Redondo, near Fort Sumner, in the arid and barren Pecos River Valley in eastern New Mexico. Bosque Redondo was a turning point for the Navajo as a people and as weavers. They were interned for five long years, an alien people in an alien and harsh world. There was not enough wool to weave into blankets or clothing. Commercial plied yarn, and commercial blankets were issued to the Navajo, who promptly raveled them to combine with the commercial yarn and a little yarn from their own sheep. The simple, bold, classic designs gave way to similar but smaller, fussier, confined arrangements of the terraced zigzags and diamonds known as Late Classic. Here, another important event took place. The government bought 4,000 Rio Grande Spanish blankets and issued them to the Navajo. With them came the seed of a totally new design concept. This style was Saltillo filtered once through Spanish-American hands and now adapted in their own fashion by the Navajo. The concentric diamonds were taken apart and made into serrate zigzag stripes. The vertical background became vertically oriented series of diamonds, and a few borders began to appear.

When the Navajo returned to their homeland in 1868, they took the new style with them. Terraced and serrate zigzag stripes and figures existed side-by-side, the serrate form gradually replacing the stepped. The government supplied them with commercial clothing and blankets, so the Navajo gradually stopped weaving for themselves. But the Navajo blanket made a splendid souvenir of army service in the West, so the Navajo wove more and more for his conquerers and less and less for himself. By 1885, blankets were being used as rugs in American homes, and so it has been ever since.

New customers, new sheep with kinky, greasy wool, and a flood of poor-quality, garish aniline dyes almost ruined Navajo weaving. A few traders, friends of the Navajo, worked toward the improvement of weaving. Commercial yarn was replaced by better-quality homespun yarn. New designs were introduced, with simple or complex borders, that reflected the white trader's taste.

From 1900 on, under the aegis of these traders, regionally distinctive patterns began to develop, and the weavers of some areas developed specialties which are easily recognized. Always, the Navajo woman injects some of her own character into these products for the American home. If, today, much of the Navajo woman's pride in her weaving has returned, the reason is not difficult to see, it is here to be seen.

# The Modern Navajo Weaver

Martin Link
Director
Navajo Tribal Museum
Window Rock, Arizona

The craft of textile manufacture is an ancient art among the Navajo Indians of the Four Corners region, but it has seen many changes throughout the centuries. Although definitely a Navajo craft, it shows influences from the ancient Pueblos, the Spanish-Mexican weavers of the Rio Grande valley, the business-minded traders of the nineteenth century, and now the fads, whimsies, and collecting habits of Anglo-Americans.

Since World War II, Navajo weaving has been exemplified by the Regional Style Period, which reflects the influence of several traders on the designs, colors, and patterns in the rugs produced in their areas. Although these area rugs are popular, they probably constitute only about twenty-five percent of the total output today; the rest being general patterns, special orders, or saddle blankets.

Navajo textiles had their greatest popularity in the 1960s, but with a national economic depression, the rapidly rising prices of Navajo rugs, a market saturated with machine-made imitations, and a decreasing consumer interest in Indian handmade crafts, the production of rugs now has declined at an alarming rate.

But all is not hopeless. The Navajo weaver has faced depressed times before and survived, and she will do it again. There are not as many weavers today as there were in the past, but they are mostly experts in their craft and very proud of their work. Although the present high prices have put Navajo rugs out of the range of many potential buyers, there still is a demand for the product from serious collectors, museums, and craft dealers. It seems that as the quantity goes down, the quality continues to rise, both in the product as well as in the individual weaver.

Many of the styles, notably the vegetal-dyed rugs from Crystal, Chinle, Wide Ruins, and recently from Burntwater, are very compatible with contemporary home designs and maintain a nation-wide popularity.

Navajo weavers, and their products, will still be around for some time to come. They will continue to be a good investment and, as always, are a beautiful manifestation of a unique craft of the First American.

**71 – Yei Rug,** Greasewood Springs
140 x 68 inches ca 1930s
Female Yeis form a colorful row on a black ground enclosed by a simple red border.

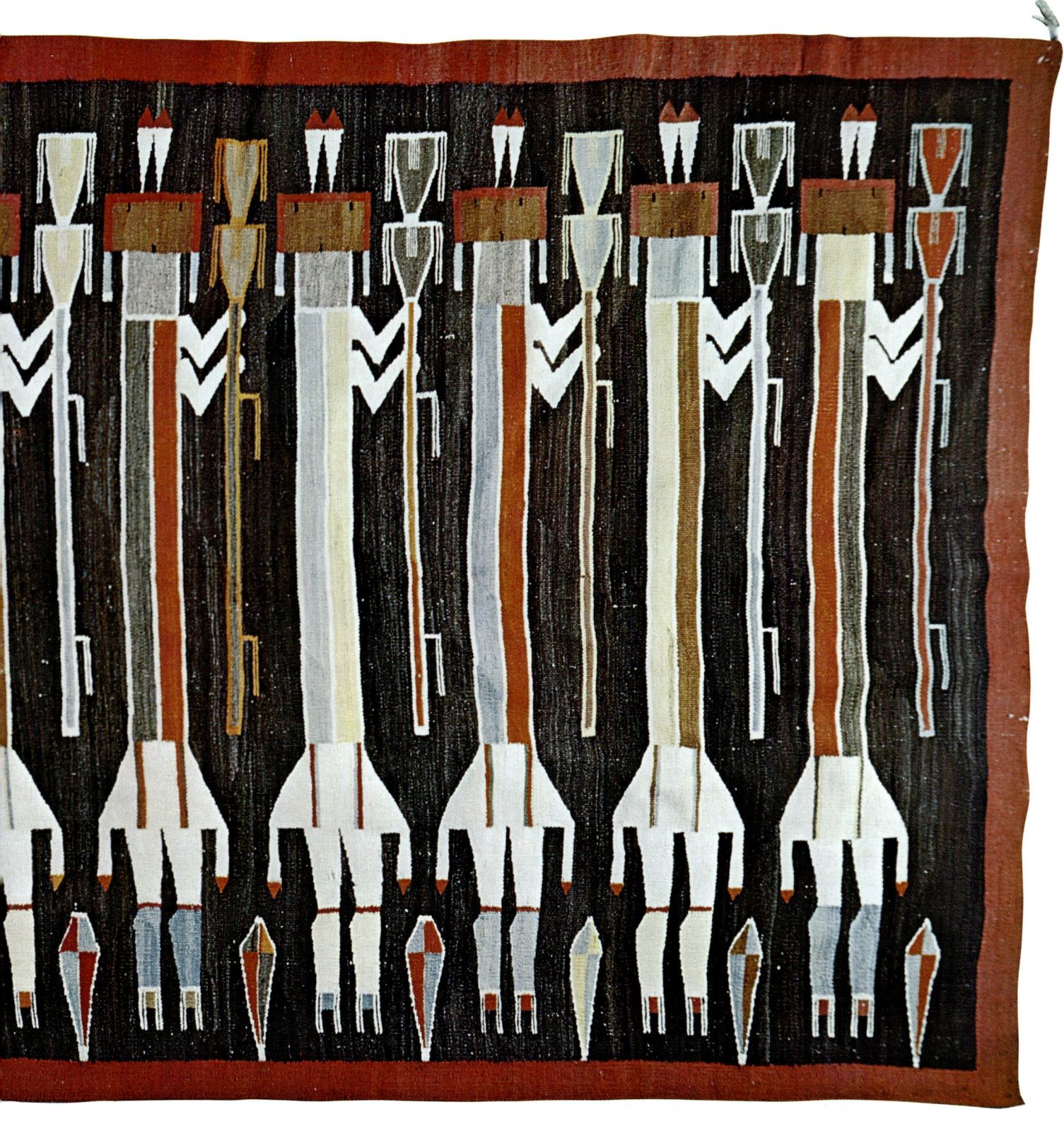

# The Other Weavers of the Southwest

Richard G. Conn, Curator
Dept. of Native Art
Denver Art Museum

There has been a long and well-developed tradition of weaving in the American Southwest; one that pre-dates the arrival of the Navajo and Apache. Fine textiles have long been a medium for native Southwest artists, and some of their earlier efforts are the most amazing.

In prehistoric times we can recognize and distinguish three important streams of culture that developed and persisted over centuries of history. The Mogollon culture centered in the forested highlands of Central Arizona and adjacent western New Mexico. It established itself early — roughly at the time of Christ. Today we remember it mostly for the imaginative ceramics it produced, such as the various Mimbres wares. However, the Mogollon people also knew how to weave and worked in various materials, such as native fibers, furs, and eventually cotton. Very little Mogollon weaving has survived and so we have little knowledge of the extent of their skills in this art. South of the highlands lies the upper reaches of the Sonoran Desert where the Hohokam people lived in prehistoric times. These industrious farmers are noted for their massive irrigation canal systems and for their city-like settlements complete with ceremonial plazas. Copper ornaments and other materials recovered from Hohokam sites show their trade connections with the more advanced native societies of Mexico. From this latter source, the Hohokam people also may have learned to weave. As was the case with the Mogollon, very few fragments of Hohokam weaving have survived to this day. And as before, we can be certain they did weave but very little else about how they did it. The Pima Indians, who are thought by some to be the modern descendants of Hohokam culture, did continue to weave cotton cloth on a limited scale. Several Army officers and Boundary Commissioners who visited the Pima in the middle 19th Century watched weavers at work, but by 1900 the art was extinct. Today very few Pima cotton textiles survive in museum collections.

The most prolific and persistent of Southwestern weavers were and are those of the great Anasazi culture; the prehistoric peoples who built Mesa Verde and Pueblo Bonito as well as their modern descendants living in the various Arizona and New Mexico Pueblos. This great stream of civilization began with groups of people who have been aptly called "the Basketmakers." While they did no true weaving, in the early centuries of this epoch they did perfect the magnificent basketry for which they will always be known. In doing so, they worked out a body of designs succeeding generations would apply to weaving. The Basketmakers did their work, both basketry and twined proto-weaving, in native fibers they could collect locally. They seem to have tested most of the plants of their homeland for use as weaving material or as dye sources. As elsewhere in the Southwest, true weaving seems to have been introduced from the South — most likely ultimately from Mexico where it was already flourishing. At some point after the simple loom and directions for using it had come into the Southwest, a new material was introduced. This was cotton, which could be grown by the settled descendants of the Basketmakers — the prehistoric Pueblo people. In time, cotton became the favored weaving fiber and the use of native plants declined.

The great days when the magnificent prehistoric sites were built and occupied is often called "The Pueblo Golden Age." This expression isn't really overblown when you compare these 11th Century Southwesterners with their contemporaries in the Old World. The Southwest had no metallurgy and no writing to be sure, but neither did they have feudalism or the Black Death. It was a dynamic time in which Pueblo arts of all kinds flourished and in which many of the most beautiful parts of historic Pueblo culture were formulated. After visiting the collection of Golden Age textiles on display at the various National Monuments of the Southwest, you might well have the impression that weavers sat down at their looms determined to explore all technical and creative possibilities. During the height of the tie-dye craze a few years ago, a ranger at Mesa Verde reported the amazement of visitors to learn that this technique had been well established there nine centuries before. And that was not all! These early Southwestern geniuses had worked out the most complex of weaving techniques including lace-like openwork and elaborate brocades. But because of its more perishable nature, fewer complete examples of these amazing works of art have survived than have of the contemporary pottery. Thus, today many people think pottery was the prehistoric Southwestern art *par excellence.*

The arrival of the Spanish in the 16th Century had two consequences for the Pueblo weavers. First, the Spanish introduced sheep and thereby wool. In time, Pueblo weavers came to use these animals' yarns as much as cotton. The second manifestation of the Spanish presence was not so fortunate. They had come, as our history books told us, looking for gold. When there was none, they looked further for whatever tribute their new domains would yield to the King's treasury. Along the Rio Grande, Spanish soldiers paid regular visits to the Pueblos and collected the best things the native had to offer: their hand-woven cotton textiles. One officer mentioned sadly that his men had almost stripped the natives bare to meet the royal demands. In such a situation, who wants to practice their most complex weaving only to have it confiscated by foreign soldiers? The Pueblo weavers quickly dropped their fine weaving and turned to simpler plain and twill weaves that could be made in enough quantity to satisfy the Spanish and clothe their families as well. So passed the great days of Pueblo textiles. Through the latter part of the 19th Century, Pueblo weavers continued to turn out cotton garments for ceremonial use and woolen textiles for bedding and everyday wear. But as silverworking and ceramics grew in economic importance, the Pueblos gradually abandoned weaving. People bought cotton garments from the conservative Hopi who maintained the art and substituted commercial woolen goods for secular needs. This is the situation today. Most of the cotton dance kilts and robes you may see worn at San Ildefonso or Cochiti were probably made by a Hopi, and the black woolen dresses are apt to be yard goods from Penneys. A few Pueblo weavers have tried to keep the art alive, but younger native craftspersons turn to more lucrative media like silver or paintings.

When one thinks of Southwestern textiles, he is apt to envision a Navajo rug or blanket first. Certainly the Navajo have created masterpieces in wool. However, let's not forget the wonderful textile accomplishments of those other Southwestern weavers and their striking works that enriched native life across the centuries.

# Technique, Tradition, and Trade,

Frederick J. Dockstader

Approximately 500 years ago, Athapascan-speaking peoples migrated from northwestern North America to the Southwest. There, they split into two major groups: the Navajo, who settled in the Utah-Colorado-Arizona-New Mexico region, and the Apache, who traveled farther south, to southern Arizona, New Mexico, western Texas, and northern Mexico. What weaving they may have brought with them is not known.

The Navajo, a more agricultural group than their Apache cousins, seem to have adapted to the cultural patterns of the Pueblo people who lived in the region. The Navajo readily took on many Pueblo activities, most particularly weaving, which was even then highly advanced. The Anasazi, the ancestors of the Pueblo, had developed the backstrap (or belt) loom several hundred years earlier. By 1000 A.D., this invention had evolved into the true loom—a standard vertical frame with heddle, tension bars, posts, and the sophisticated forms necessary for advanced textile production. The Navajo could thereby take advantage of the latest state of the art, building from there.

And build they did. Few peoples have taken on a new art form, practiced it with vigor, and surpassed their teachers as remarkably as did the Navajo. Just as they later learned to work silver from watching itinerant Mexican blacksmiths and saddle-makers, developing the craft into a new tradition, so too did they take the Pueblo loom and carry it to greater heights of productivity. They quickly discovered that raw materials were readily available: animal and plant fibers, plant and mineral dyestuffs, and wood for the few weaving tools needed. These materials were blended to make sleeping covers, blankets, and garments which, though copied from the Pueblo styles, soon came to have a distinctly Navajo sense of design. They also made one major change, why we do not know. Whereas among the Pueblo folk, men did the weaving, this art was placed in the capable hands of Navajo women, where it remains today.

We have little knowledge of Pueblo weaving of the early period, but we do know that it was plentiful, and we have some idea of the forms it took. Belting, blankets, wrap-around garments, and mantles were all part of the weaver's production. The fragmentary material evidence does not allow a detailed analysis of type, style, or quantity of production.

With the entry of the European into the Southwest in the mid-16th Century, all this changed almost overnight. The introduction of domestic sheep had a more profound impact upon the Navajo weaver than it did on the Pueblo people. While adopting sheep's wool as a weaving material, the Pueblo seem never to have abandoned cotton, nor digressed from traditional and conventional weaving patterns. When the Navajos began weaving, approximately 1650, they produced only limited amounts of cotton blankets. More remarkably, they switched to a wide loom although they continued to use the narrow belt loom in a limited way. As a result, the Pueblo weavers, particularly the Hopi, became the traditional suppliers of narrow loom items to the Navajo. The Navajo's switch to a new material and true loom had only slight effect upon weaving techniques.

The old belt loom, the precursor of the true loom, was well-suited to the narrow-strip forms of weaving. Once the raw materials were collected, they had to be cleansed and the fibers aligned. By beating and carding, the fibers were brushed, cleaned, and pulled together in a parallel direction. The beater was usually a several-pronged, fan-shaped implement. The "cards" originally were rough-surfaced objects (cactus was a helpful accessory), but gave way in time to complex toothed implements. Today, pairs of metal-tined cards are most commonly employed.

Once carded, the fibers were twisted for strength into long threads, with a smooth, even diameter. This process could be done laboriously by hand or by means of a mechanical aid, such as a spindle, which allowed tighter twisting hence greater strength. Spindles were composed of round, wooden rods of approximately 2 feet long, 3/8 inches in diameter, which were initially attached by winding them around the shaft. Fibers added to the shaft, rotated by the fingers, blended with the previous lengths, producing an ever-lengthening thread. To maintain an even rotation, a balance-wheel was added. This "spindle-whorl" provided momentum and a more even, tightly twisted thread. These discs are approximately 3-1/2 inches in diameter. Threads created by this twisting are commonly referred to as S-twist and Z-twist, due to their appearance when viewed vertically. The S-twist is common in the Americas, however the Z-twist is more usually found in Southwestern textiles.

Just as the textile is the sum of its parts, so too is the thread forming the textile. It is the product of hundreds and thousands of tiny, short fibers of varying lengths, interlocked by spinning to yield a thread lengthy enough to weave. Indeed, weaving itself is but the further interlocking of these tightly-spun threads.

The belt loom is simply a long "ring" of cording, wrapped around two poles stretched apart, and employs few implements. In use, one rod, the "warp beam," is attached to an overhead tree limb or pole, or to a stationary wall. The rod nearest the weaver, the "breast beam," is attached to a wide strap or belt which is fastened around the weaver's body, hence the term "belt loom" or "backstrap loom." The two major rods are joined to each other by the warp, which is wound back and forth to form the "ring" warp. The weaver, working either from a sitting or kneeling position, keeps the warp taut by the tension of body position, increasing or decreasing it by moving slightly forward or backward.

Although this technique is familiar in the Southwest, most Pueblo weavers have not used the waist principle for centuries. Rather, their loom is approached vertically. The loom poles are fastened to the ceiling and to blocks or anchors set securely in the floor. The loom employs a heddle, usually a simple rod with string loops, each of which holds a warp thread. As the heddle is pulled toward the weaver, all attached threads are separated from the main warp. The weft thread can then be inserted through the opening or "shed" provided by the rod. A batten (or sword), the flat polished stick that opens the warp, is inserted and turned sideways. It also beats down, or battens, the weave to tighten it. A small comb is also used for this purpose by many weavers.

The shuttle rod, or bobbin, is not essential. Many weavers simply use their fingers to insert the weft thread and work it along the fabric. The shed rod is then pulled down to bring other warp threads forward. These few basic implements allow the skilled weaver an almost unlimited variety of textures and patterns.

Raising the warp threads by means of the heddle allows the weaver to insert weft threads in a prearranged combination so as to produce the desired design. Color changes are readily introduced by using different colored weft threads. The weaver proceeds upwards, with the finished weave pulled behind the loom to bring the next section forward.

Some time after this loom became common, weavers saw that despite its light weight, easy mobility, and ready control over production, the belt loom had serious drawbacks. It was not well-suited to the production of wide sections of cloth. Textiles had to be sewn together to provide blankets, a nuisance that also caused bumpy, irregular seams.

The obvious answer was a larger, heavier loom. This option, however, required far greater tension than the weaver could provide by body strength, nor could firm weaving be handled at more than arm's length. At some time during this period, the wide loom came into existence—whether as a long development, or the overnight inspiration of some anonymous genius, we will never know. By 1000 A.D. in the Southwest, the custom was widespread of setting two large loom poles (or using trees) vertically, upon which the loom beams were fastened horizontally, tightly bound with heavy cording to provide the needed framing. These horizontal beams were in turn fastened to tension rods at the upper and lower extensions. Warp thread was wound around the rods as loosely or closely as desired. The true loom did not really change in form or technical arrangement from the belt loom in other than size and its more rigid, permanent construction. Heddle and shed rods were retained, as was a larger batten, but the body of the weaver was now entirely free. The weaver could sit or kneel in front of the loom, working from the bottom upwards, as before (see illustration). By moving back and forth, the weaver could maintain a straight level weave. However, some weavers ultimately found it easier to sit in one place and weave upwards as far as the arms could conveniently reach. This produced a gradually tapering triangular area of woven fabric, requiring the weaver to move to one side or the other to complete the missing sections. The oblique join-line created by this technique is the familiar "lazy line" found so commonly in Navajo weaving, rarely however in Pueblo weaving.

The new loom allowed far larger textiles and higher productivity, assets which readily outweighed the lack of mobility. The increase in quantity both enhanced weaving's importance in the economic life of the people and affected their costume. Experimentation followed in color, texture, and design motifs, as complex weaves were achieved. Sheep's wool was easier than cotton to weave, since it was firmer and locked together better, yielding stronger threads. The introduction of aniline dyes in 1870 made a whole new color palette available. Unfortunately, in time this resulted in

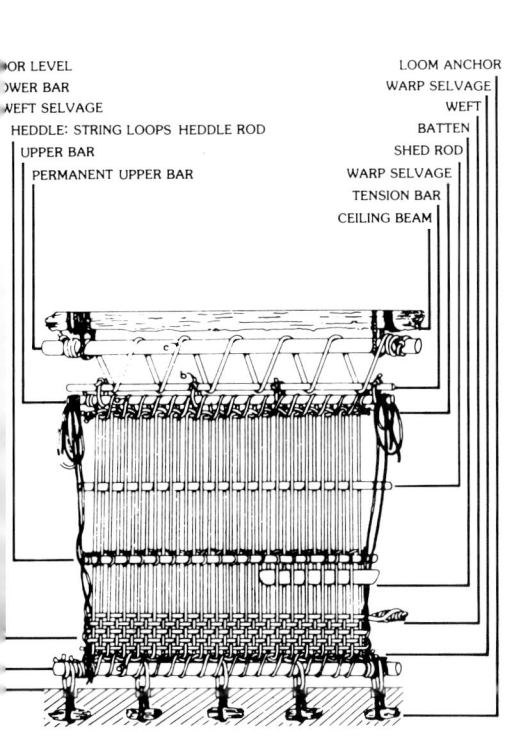

the kaleidoscopic "eye dazzlers" of the Germantown commercial yarn period, which replaced the softer vegetal-dye coloring. Aniline dyes were easily prepared and were preferred by many weavers and not a few white purchasers.

As for variety of weave, there seems not to have been a great amount of experimentation undertaken by Navajo weavers of the period. They seem to have been more concerned with design, which did undergo remarkable novelties. Much of this was the work of the weavers themselves, but a great influence came from Indian traders who sought to keep up the quality of the weave while at the same time finding ways to make the products more attractive and desirable to their white customers. Many of the designs selected were taken from Oriental patterns popular with white settlers of the 1880-1910 era, from which has come the now-accepted "traditional" Navajo weaving forms. These pressures, combined with ready-made cotton warp, pre-dyed weft, and a large-scale demand for textiles, caused an inevitable decline in quality of native dyed wool and it was a rare trader who concerned himself with efforts to maintain standards.

Some did, however, and out of this early concern, as well as later efforts on the part of devoted Indian and white individuals, came the revival of interest and quality which continues to the present time. But this revival had to surmount the crossfire of cultural and economic forces which threatened for a time to destroy the art. The replacement of a native market and cultural purpose, together with costumer resistance to paying more than token amounts for weaving, caused women to abandon the loom in large numbers. The economic role of weaving became exploitative. In the past, exchange—or barter—had been largely between peoples of similar traditions and interests, even though many consumers were actually tourists from distant villages. These outside demands did affect local weavers, but minimally. Europeans, on the other hand, introduced totally new needs, interests, and demands. Previously, weaving for native needs had been for body coverings and sleeping blankets. The white settler, by and large, had little interest in these. He wanted wall hangings, floor rugs, heavyweight blankets, and different colors and designs.

Where the weaver had once received commensurate income through mutually satisfactory trade avenues, the ethnically-affected reaction of the whites, coupled with a religious, social, and cultural disregard, not only lessened the weavers' financial income, but more importantly, depleted their artistic pride and self-respect. Inevitably, quality declined, in turn depressing prices. At one time, Navajo weavers were paid for their work by the pound, a system almost totally divorced from the textile's intrinsic and aesthetic value. Thirty cents a pound for average work to a dollar for the best weaving was the "going rate."

Yet, the art refused to die out. When an upturn in interest made itself felt, there were weavers to respond. Interestingly, where previously the fact that ninety-five percent of the customers for Navajo weaving were white, had been a serious problem, this market concentration now became its salvation. The interest, of course was different. Consumers were interested in quality and willing to pay for superior work. Variety was sought after, a return to traditional forms and color patterns applauded, and the weavers began slowly to assert themselves in their work. Improved quality and innovation were the results.

One of the few truly "new" techniques was the so-called "raised outline" technique developed in the Coalmine Mesa area of Arizona in the mid-1960's. Other innovations were finer threads, resulting in tighter weaves, greater experimentation in linear patterns and color schemes, and remarkably complex designs. Some of these are, unfortunately, reminiscent of the crazy-quilt period of the eye-dazzlers.

As with the Pueblo weavers, the Navajo people found their work eagerly sought after, particularly after museums began to include special weaving exhibits in their programs, accepting Indian textiles as a true art form. This development had a momentous impact. The exhibitions were not only successful from the institutional point of view, but since many of them were accompanied by opportunities for the visitors to purchase textiles in museum shops, familiarity spread, resulting in an ever-widening demand for the products of the Indian loom.

Remarkably, this overwhelming enthusiasm did not lessen quality. Weavers responded with even greater fidelity. In many ethnic arts fields, quality often declines with quantity production, particularly when the purchaser is non-native. With Navajo weaving, it can safely be said that the product of the Southwestern loom today is easily equal to anything produced in the past, and sometimes superior. Not only have the financial rewards been sufficient to encourage the better weavers to achieve maximum quality in design and style, but even the average weavers enjoy a new sense of purpose.

There have undeniably been some adverse effects of this increase in interest. There is still a great disproportion between the weaver's income and time spent in preparation and weaving. Another equally serious problem has been the recent competition from non-Indian handwoven textiles, made in replica of Navajo designs and styles. Most of the better examples of this counterfeit weave originate in Oaxaca, Mexico although some have been made in the Orient. While the experienced eye can detect the copy, the layman can be fairly easily fooled. They are, after all, hand-woven, the colors are fairly close to the originals, and the motifs are mirror copies of typical Navajo weaving.

Nevertheless, the future of Navajo weaving is unquestionably bright. While the total number of weavers may be fewer than in the past, these craftsmen are more conscious of the demand for high standards and are meeting it. More and more white consumers are becoming interested in including Navajo textiles in their home decor. More importantly, Indian people themselves are increasingly "going back to old times" in their desire to acquire traditional art for their own social and ceremonial needs. That the old times will never return is less important than is the concern of the people for their own products. With these forces combining to create a vital, active art, there will be demand for good quality textiles as long as there are Navajo weavers.

**16**     **Wedge Weave**
       64 x 66 inches ca 1875

Sometime after the Navajo returned to their homeland from Bosque Redondo, they developed the loom technique usually called wedge weave (sometimes called pulled warp). In this variation of plain tapestry weave, the wefts were inserted at an angle to the verticle warps, resulting in a series of diagonal stripes frequently separated by bands of plain tapestry. When the blanket was cut free from the loom the tension caused by placing the wefts diagonally was released, pulling the warp out of line and giving the edge a scalloped appearance. This technique died out about 1900.

    This orange, red and olive green Wedge Weave is mostly hand spun of Germantown four-ply yarn made with aniline dyes. This very fine example is of the over-all variety in which the zig-zag patterns are arranged to form vertical stripes. The warp is wool. In the 1880's, Wedge Weaves were made around Fort Defiance, in the eastern section of Navajo country. Essentially, this design comes from that area, although one type is from the San Luis Valley.

**17**     **Wedge Weave**
       78 x 57 inches ca 1890

Hand-spun wool, with an all-over pattern, this Wedge Weave has a cotton string warp and is made with aniline dyes. The dark purple color, faded to gray, plus the use of cotton warp, is the principal indicator which dates this piece around the 1890's.

**30**     **Diyugi Wearing Blanket**
       80 x 52 inches ca 1880

The dyes are a combination of native vegetal dyes and aniline—the reds being aniline, the yellows, browns, and tans being native vegetal dyes. The design is that of the Spider Woman Cross, Spider Woman being the person who taught the Navajos to weave in legend. This is a decorative motif which came into being around 1870 and lasted until about 1890. It has quite a few "lazy lines" and is very softly woven. It would have draped well as a wearing blanket.

17

30

# The Early Period

**1 — Woman's Shoulder Blanket**
53 x 66 inches  ca 1860
Women's blankets were made in the Pueblo tradition, characterized by narrow alternating stripes, but with decorative end and center panels added to enhance their beauty. Natural wood color stripes alternate with indigo blue, while the red was raveled from imported Bayeta cloth.

30  Early Navajo weaving apparel originated in Pueblo weaving modified by Spanish weaving and made completely Navajo by their own creative genius. Early Pueblo garments were wider than long, and were of solid dark color or decorated only with simple stripes. Spanish blankets were woven in tapestry weave, longer than wide, and decorated with stripes of brown, white, or indigo blue, often clustered in zones to lend more interest to the simple decorative device. The Navajo adopted and changed each of these traditions, and by the mid 1800s they had created distinctive garments based on each — the shoulder blanket, the dress, and the sarape.

**2 — Woman's Dress** (half)
51 x 34 inches ca 1860
From the Pueblo one-piece dark wool dress the Navajo woman evolved the two-piece dress, dark center but made decorative by indigo blue designs on red raveled cloth panels at each end.

**3 — Old Rio Grande**
88 x 51 inches ca 1875
All-over striped patterns such as this were characteristic of the majority of Old Rio Grande blankets. The color scheme of warm reds, pinks, and yellows alternating with natural brown wool shows the sophistication which can be achieved by simple means.

**4 — Old Rio Grande Sarape**
102 x 52 inches ca 1850
The decoration in this blanket consists entirely of finely balanced zones of stripes in natural brown wool on a plain white ground. Some of the stripes are bordered by beading, a technique in which wefts of white and brown are woven so as to produce small blocks of alternating colors.

**5 — Spanish (Old Rio Grande) Sarape**
76 x 51 inches ca 1850-75
Natural white wool warp fringes, natural brown weft, and indigo blue clustered stripes in tapestry weave made this Old Rio Grande Spanish prototype of the early Navajo sarape. Woven in two pieces and sewn together.

2

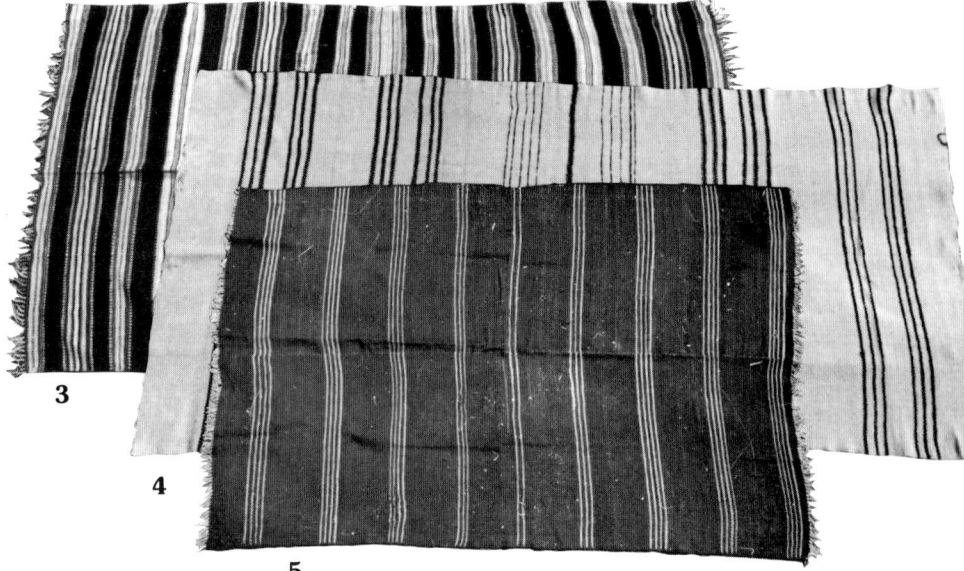

3

4

5

7

**6 — Old Rio Grande Jerga (herga) cloth** *(not illustrated)*
169 x 52 inches  ca 1875
Lengths of plaid cloth in a plain twill weave were sewed together and used as carpets or wall hangings, covers for pack loads, mattress covers, large bags, or anything else that was needed. The cloth was also cut and tailored into rough but warm clothing. The color patterns, especially the lavender, mark it as Old Rio Grande.

**7 — "Moki Pattern" Wearing Blanket**
68 x 60 inches  ca 1875
Popularly called Moki or Hopi style blankets, these were copied from Spanish-American blankets. The vertical serrate diamonds are derived from Saltillo patterns. The red yarns are raveled from aniline-dyed soft American flannel.

**8 — Wearing Blanket**
75 x 54 inches  ca 1875
Soft-woven all-purpose borderless blanket with zones of serrate zigzag stripes on combed pink ground made by carding together white wool and raveled soft-woven red flannel of American manufacture. Combed pink was characteristic of the mid-1870s. Such blankets served as overcoat, bed blanket, and, folded, as a carrying bag.

**9 — Rug**
53 x 34 inches  ca 1885-1900
Zigzag stripes in various colors combine to form horizontal band of diamonds and triangles with diagonal pattern join, all enclosed in a compound border.

**10 — Old Rio Grande Sarape**
80 x 50 inches  ca 1880
Soft-woven two-piece blanket sewn together at center. Design of zoned stripes in reds, lavenders, brown, and white, is enclosed by complex side borders with vertical serrate zigzag edges.

**11 — Rug  Southern Reservation**
87 x 50 inches  ca 1900
The Saint Andrews Cross design with terraced outline and dentate edges, woven in neutral colors of white, brown, and tan made by carding together brown and white, is typical of turn of the century rugs woven for "Back East homes".

# Bosque Redondo and After

About 1865, while the Navajo were interned at Bosque Redondo on the arid plains of New Mexico, many changes occurred in their weaving. New aniline-dyed commercial yarns, cloth, and blankets, were issued to them, which they combined with wool from their few sheep, into Late Classic blankets. In terms of design, they came face to face with the style developed in Saltillo, Mexico, in the 1700s and introduced to and simplified by the Spanish Old Rio Grande weavers after 1800. The Navajo eagerly adopted the Saltillo style but modified it in proper Navajo fashion. By 1885 it had almost replaced the old terraced zigzag Classic style.

**12 — Navajo, Late Classic**
68 x 52 inches  ca 1865-70
The Saltillo serrate diamond motif interpreted as Navajo zigzag stripes. Although the design uses diagonal serrate layout, the color changes in this blanket are still done in small steps or terraces. The color scheme, with its raveled red cloth ground end designs in indigo blue, indigo over native yellow dye, and natural white, reflect the Navajo concept of color scheme.

**13 — Old Rio Grande Blanket**
86 x 49 inches  ca 1850-70
The Saltillo diamond figure in this blanket has been simplified, coarsened, and adapted to a band pattern. Each decorative band consists of the central section of a concentric serrate diamond motif truncated top and bottom by zones of clustered stripes. The color scheme is typical of the natural dyes of the Rio Grande Valley.

**14 — Saltillo Sarape**
*(not illustrated)*
95 x 53 inches  ca 1750
The Saltillo Sarape is a full classic piece, made around 1750, showing the skilled spinning, dying, and loom work characteristic of the finest pieces of their kind. This was the type of thing which influenced, first, Spanish-American weaving, and then, after 1865, Navajo weaving. All of the new designs which are found in the figures on this piece were enlarged, coarsened, and carried over into Spanish-American, and later, Navajo weaving.

12

13

**15 — Saltillo Sarape, Mexico**
 95 x 52 inches  ca 1775-1825
Fine weaving and superb design characterize this Saltillo sarape with its central motif of concentric serrate diamonds, its minutely figured vertically oriented background, and the figured border. Such blankets were the design source for the Spanish weavers of the Rio Grande Valley and, in turn, the Navajo. The subtle colors reflect the Saltillo mastery of natural dyestuffs.

# Pan-Reservation Rug Styles

Navajo blankets became Navajo rugs about 1885. These early rugs were woven in the various styles known to the Navajo, for once a pattern was adopted it continued to be used from then on. Today's rugs may be made in patterns which date back to 1800, to 1865, or to one which was created last week. Elements of different styles are often combined. This vast reservoir of Navajo design combined with the Navajo woman's creative ability have produced many tens of thousands of textiles, none of which are exactly alike.

**18 — Rug**
  57 x 44 inches ca 1890-1910
Broad Meander pattern stripes in white (or faded yellow?) on red ground, separated by black and gray stripes. This pattern resembles the common wearing blanket of the 1860s.

**19 — Rug**
  72 x 53 inches ca 1910
Vertical rows of Saltillo diamonds in red, black, and gray on white ground, enclosed by a wide positive-negative border in red and black, emphasized by white outline stripe. Probably Crystal area.

**20 — Chief Pattern Rug**
  50 x 51 inches ca 1940s
Rug made in Chief blanket pattern of 1860. Broad black and white striped ground with end and center decorative panels overlaid with nine blocks done in red with inlaid diamond stripes derived from Saltillo sources.

**21 — Chief Pattern Rug**
  50 x 67 inches ca 1950
Man's shoulder blanket pattern of 1800, with broad black and white striped ground overlaid with modified Saltillo serrate diamonds in red. The proportions are Pueblo in origin.

**22 — Rug**
  42 x 22 inches 1960s
Pair of nearly identical rugs derived from the woman's traditional two-piece dress in red, green, and pink on a black ground.

### 23 – Rug
55 x 38 inches  ca 1910
Pattern in diamond stripes in red, white, black, gray, and tan, so arranged as to form a Saint Andrew's cross design.

### 24 – Rug
70 x 44 inches  ca 1900
Central motif of derived Saltillo diamonds in black, white, and brown on ground of wide red and gray stripes.

### 25 – Rug
63 x 39 inches  ca 1930
Broad stripes of gray and black decorated by modified diamond stripes in red and white.

### 26 – Pan-reservation Style Rug
76 x 37 inches  ca 1900
Row after row of diamond stripes in black, red, brown, and gray form a simple but lively pattern. Even the border is toothed to carry out the all-over serrate pattern.

### 27 – Pan-reservation Style Rug
37 x 26 inches  Modern
A simple, restrained vertical alignment of diamond figures in black and white on a red ground surrounded by compound vertical serrate borders marks this sophisticated small textile.

### 28 – Chief Pattern Rug
49 x 57 inches  ca 1890
Rug combining the old "Chief" pattern with corner and center "spots" of Saltillo serrate diamonds.

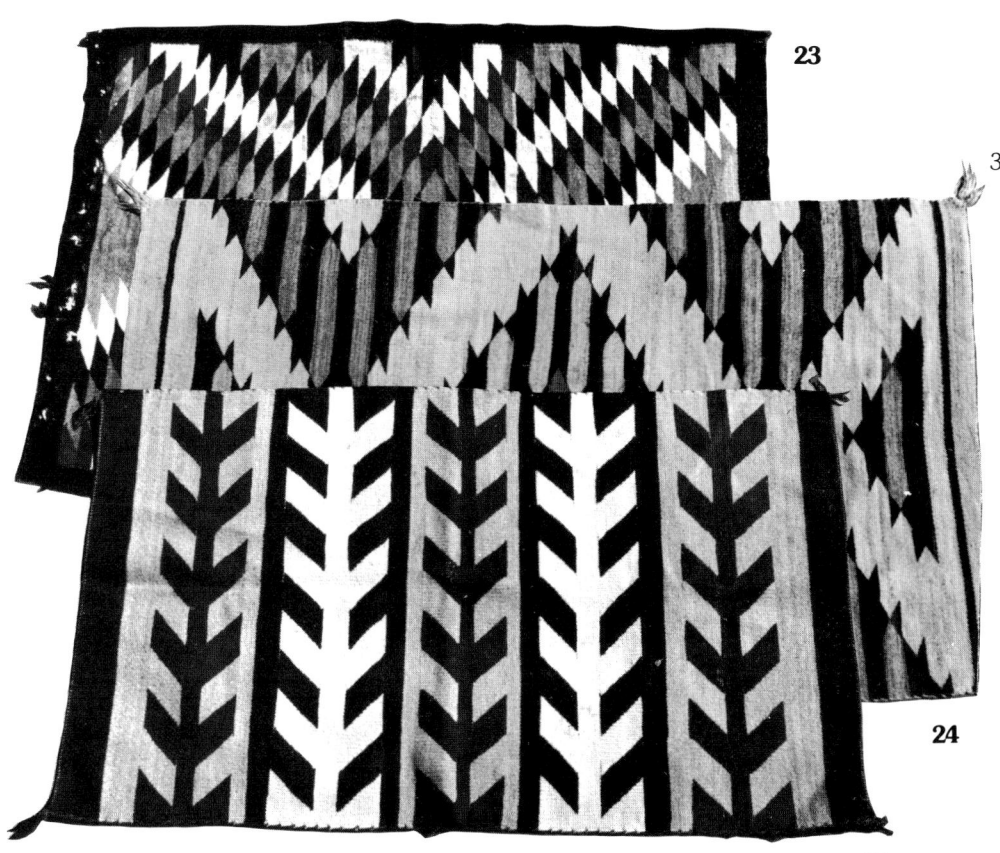

**29 — Rug**
57 x 38 inches  1900-1910
Concentric serrate diamonds arranged in an all-over pattern in black, white, and red on a gray ground. Outlining in a contrasting color was once common in Navajo weaving. Probably Teec Nos Pos area.

# Germantown Blankets

33

32

At Bosque Redondo the Navajo were introduced to a fine 3-ply commercial wool yarn dyed in the then new aniline colors made in the eastern United States and named after Germantown, Pennsylvania. About 1875, 4-ply yarns of the same kind were introduced. Because of their fine texture and wide color range, Germantown yarns lent themselves to fine weaving and infinite detail in the hands of the Navajo. Combined with the new Saltillo design, they led to the development of the complex and colorful Eye-dazzlers of the mid-1880s. Every kind of textile woven in native-spun wool was also produced in Germantown yarns, but these yarns are especially associated with the Eye-dazzler blankets, saddle throws, fancy rugs, table runners, and pillow tops. Except for small curio pieces, Germantown yarn weaving died out about 1900.

**31 — Rug** *(illustrated on page 39)*
93 x 68 inches  ca 1900
Moki (Hopi) pattern variant with broad stripes of black faded to green, faded dark blue with Red displaying piece pipes, bows and arrows and tomahawk. The wool used from sick and dead sheep is very harsh and is called kemp (fibers) and was primarily used in the manufacturing of carpet. This four-ply analine dyed Germantown yarn was introduced to the Navajos about 1902 and very few rugs were ever produced because of the type of yarn which makes the rug a rarity.

**32 — Germantown "Eye Dazzler"**
85 x 48 inches  ca 1885
Vertical rows of concentric Saltillo serrate diamonds surrounded by a serrate closed border in several colors on a red ground mark this typical Eye Dazzler blanket.

**33 — Germantown Table Runner**
72 x 18 inches  ca 1900
Finely woven table runner with sewn-on fringes is typical of early curio pieces with vertical row of serrate Saltillo diamond and serrate border.

**34 – Germantown Pictorial**
72 x 41 inches  ca 1880
Small, early style human figures combined with central serrate Saltillo diamond, geometric and panels, and open corner borders, make this a typical early Germantown blanket.

**31 — Rug**

93 x 68 inches  ca 1900

Moki (Hopi) pattern variant with broad stripes of black faded to green, faded dark blue with Red displaying piece pipes, bows and arrows and tomahawk. The wool used from sick and dead sheep is very harsh and is called kemp (fibers) and was primarily used in the manufacturing of carpet. This four-ply analine dyed Germantown yarn was introduced to the Navajos about 1902 and very few rugs were ever produced because of the type of yarn which makes the rug a rarity.

# Ganado Area

With the advent of the railroad, commercial blankets and clothing, poor sheep, and poor aniline dyes about 1880, Navajo weaving suffered a decline. Lorenzo Hubbell, pioneer trader of Ganado, Arizona, helped the Navajo to improve their weaving and to increase their rug sales by introducing characteristics of broader appeal to Anglo housewives. He introduced the neutral gray ground that would not clash with Victorian interiors. He had his favorite rug designs, replete with crosses in all styles, painted so that customers could select a pattern that would be modified only slightly in the weaving. He pioneered the large rug for large rooms, the hall and stair runners, and paired door curtains. His favorite color was the dark red now known as Ganado Red. His 300 weavers produced rugs which were sold by mail and through the Fred Harvey establishments. He initiated the great Indian Curio Trade of the Southwest and the first well-known regional style.

### 35 — Ganado Rug
78 x 39 inches  ca 1910-20
Terraces, outlined diamonds, combined with serrate diamonds, in black, gray, tan, and red, on a white ground framed by terraced zigzag and simple border in tan and black.

### 36 — Ganado Rug
54 x 35 inches  ca 1900
Interlace trellis pattern in red, black, and gray on white ground, surrounded by a massive Greek fret border in black and gray.

### 37 — Ganado Rug
63 x 36 inches  ca 1910
Large, bold central diamond motif with terraced edges and hooks, with small checkerboard diamond in center, combined with triangles, vertical diamond, and a figured border with "spear" heads.

**38 — Ganado Rug**
62 x 43 inches ca 1890-1900
The interlace trellis or lattice pattern in red, tan, and black on a white ground. C. N. Cotton published this pattern in 1896.

**39 — Ganado Rug**
82 x 60 inches  1900-1910
Large cross and box figures dominate the rug, mostly in muted grays and white emphasized with red. The zigzag diamond stripes and the small stacked triangles are derived from Saltillo.

**40 — Ganado Rug**
80 x 50 inches  ca 1890-1900
Classic-derived terraced zigzag stripes and diamonds in red, pink, black, and white, combined with crosses and small vertical devices derived from Saltillo on a neutral gray ground. Simple borders in red and black.

**41 — Ganado Rug**
45 x 87 inches  ca 1900
Saltillo serrate diamonds in red and black, combined with central cross on gray and white ground, bordered in black, white, and gray. Short, wide rug, probably for a hallway.

**42 — Ganado Rug**
86 x 54 inches  ca 1910
Vertical diamond rows and crosses in black and white on a gray ground enclosed by a meander border in black and white. Similar rugs were made at Crystal.

**43 — Ganado Rug**
133 x 66 inches  ca 1920s
The red and black compound border in alternating opposed terraced triangles encloses a design made of stepped-edge triangles in red, black, and white, based along the sides and ends, and meeting at the center to form a St. Andrew's Cross.

**44 — Ganado Rug**
67 x 43 inches  ca 1900-1910
Early rug combining vertical rows of serrate diamonds with swastikas introduced by the traders, all enclosed in a plain border.

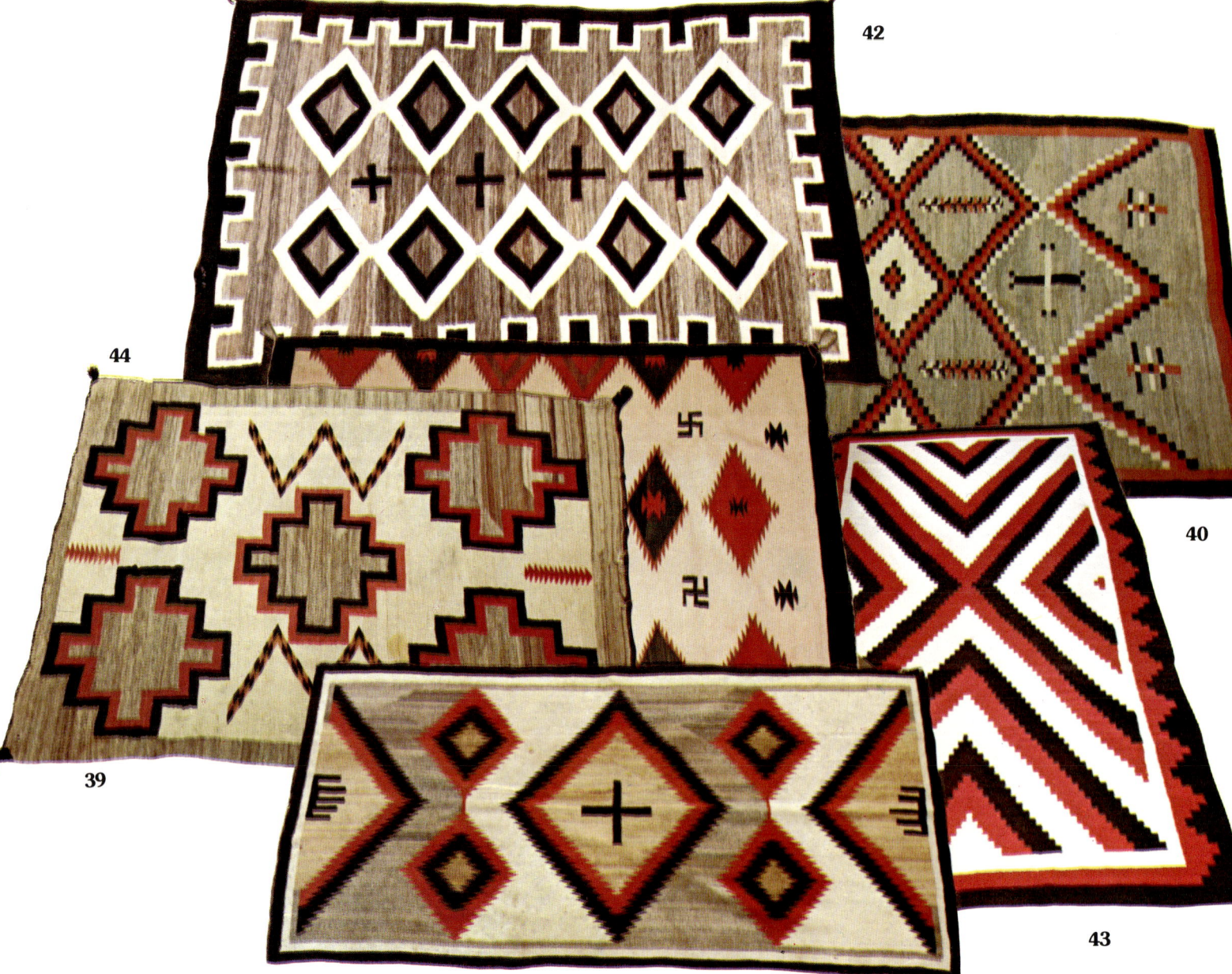

# Klagetoh

**45 – Klagetoh Rug**
101 x 60 inches ca 1910
Elaborate version of terraced diamonds with flags at corners and crosses in center enclosed by multiple-figured border. Red, black, and white on gray ground.

Klagetoh lies south of Ganado in eastern Arizona. The weaving of this area was strongly influenced by that of Ganado, particularly in the use of neutral-colored grounds and strong, bold, geometric design motifs.

**46 — Klagetoh Rug**
62 x 38 inches  ca 1930
Bold variation of vertical terraced diamonds and parallel terraced zigzag stripes framed by multiple borders in white, black, and red.

**47 — Klagetoh Rug**
55 x 30 inches  ca 1920
Vertically symmetrical figures in black, white, and red on a gray ground. Positive-negative border in red and black.

**48 — Klagetoh Rug**
68 x 46 inches  ca 1900
Vertically symmetrical arrangement of large terraced diamonds in Ganado Red on gray ground formed by multiple-figured borders in red, black, white, and gray.

**49 — Klagetoh**
152 x 98 inches  ca 1910
Woven of the natural colors black, brown, gray and white, with an addition of red. Has a large serrated diamond center. Border and all of the outlines have a serrated edge.

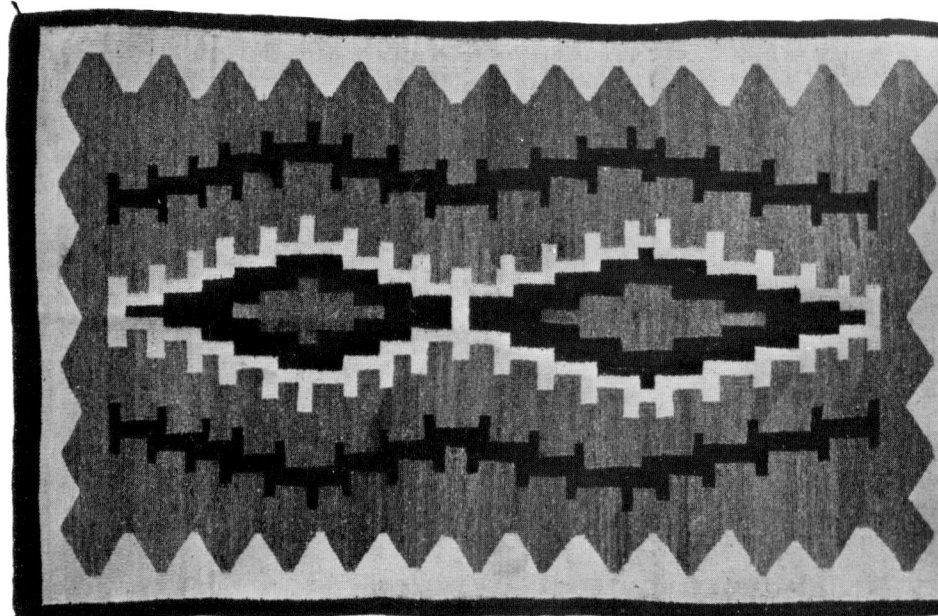

46

47

49

48

# Two Gray Hills

Two Gray Hills lies on the eastern slope of the Chuska Mountains in western New Mexico. About 1915, some of the Crystal area designs were taken over here, all done in natural colors. The various shades of gray and brown are achieved by combing together wool from "black" and white sheep in different proportions. Emphasis today is on fine weaving, at which the Two Gray Hills weavers excel.

**50 — Two Gray Hills Tapestry**
34 x 22 inches  Modern
Small, finely woven tapestry with beadworklike design in typical natural-colored wool yarns. Two Gray Hills tapestries are among the finest fabrics woven by the Navajo today.

**51 — Small Natural Wool Tapestry**
37 x 24 inches  Recent
Simple modern tapestry with paired 8-pointed star design done in white outline accented in brown on tan ground. These are traditional Two Gray Hills colors but the design is not so complex as most.

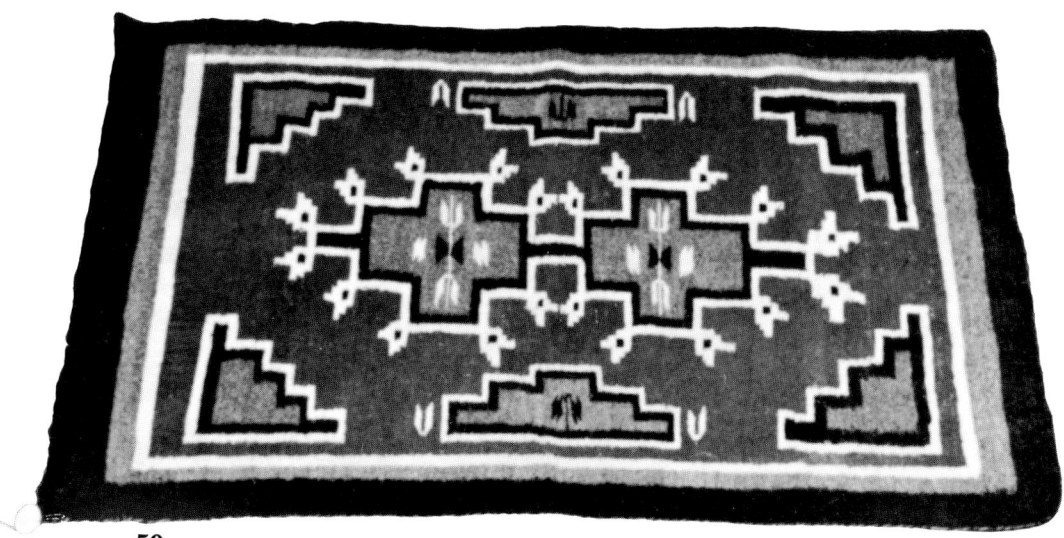

50

51

**52 — Two Gray Hills Rug**
100 x 60 inches  ca 1925
The complex design and fine proportions are achieved by the use of black, white, and two shades of tan natural-colored wools. Framed by a single fretted border inside a plain border.

# Crystal

Crystal is in the extreme western edge of New Mexico, north of Gallup. In 1896, Crystal Post was bought by J. B. Moore, who, like Hubbell, tried to improve Navajo weaving and to promote Navajo rugs for American homes. To this end, he developed a production-line weaving industry. He sent local wool east to be cleaned. When it came back, he had his best spinners spin the wool into yarn, which his wife then dyed with superior aniline dyes in her own kitchen. The ready-dyed yarn was then issued to his best weavers, who wove rugs in slightly varied, standardized patterns in whatever size and color-scheme his mail-order customers might choose. He copied Classic designs but also combined Oriental rug motifs with beadwork patterns and some of his own invention. These were made up into color plates and catalogues, widely distributed so that customers could order what they wanted. His Crystal pattern rugs are highly distinctive and one Crystal variety served as the source of Two Gray Hills design.

**53 — Crystal Rug**
81 x 55 inches  ca 1910
Simple design with a central motif of arrow-tipped crosses and hour-glass figures in dull red and black on gray ground surrounded by a diamond-figured border in white, red and black.

**54 — Crystal Rug**
90 x 54 inches  ca 1910
A typical Moore Crystal, combining swastikas and crosses of Oriental origin with "pine beetle" designs of his own devising in the corners. The lacy fringes on the geometric side patterns are typical. Black, white, tan, and red on gray. Plain borders.

**55 — Crystal Rug**
86 x 54 inches  ca 1910
A vertical composition of concentric diamonds and central rectangles framed by terraced zigzag along sides, all embellished with corner flags or pothooks. Black, white, tan, and red, with simple black and white border.

**56 — Crystal Rug**
88 x 57 inches  ca 1910
Elaborate arrangement of small unrelated elements, some spotted asymmetrically within the figured border. Colors are black, white, tan, and red, on gray ground.

**57 — Crystal Rug**
89 x 48 inches  ca 1925
Very elaborate rug with symmetrically arranged large terraced crosses with flatted corners surrounded by several serrate zigzag and diamond elements and feathers, all confined by a narrow simple border. Red, black, gray, and tan on white ground. The feather motif is common in the Shiprock area.

**58 — Crystal Rug**
69 x 41 inches  ca 1910
A modified Saint Andrew's Cross in red and white with serrate edges on a gray ground, flanked by smaller serrate and terraced elements framed by a simple red and black border.

**59 — Crystal or Ganado Rug**
67 x 37 inches  ca 1910
A "Fancy Grade" early rug with design of vertically stacked concentric diamonds, each bordered by a fret pattern, all included within multiple borders, plain and figured. Such pieces, the apex in early rug trade, were marked by fine weaving and complex design.

**60 — Crystal Rug** (not illustrated)
82 x 61 inches  ca 1930s
Concentric serrate diamonds and Roman crosses in gray and black on white angora wool ground make this a striking rug. A figured border in black and white triangles completes the design.

57

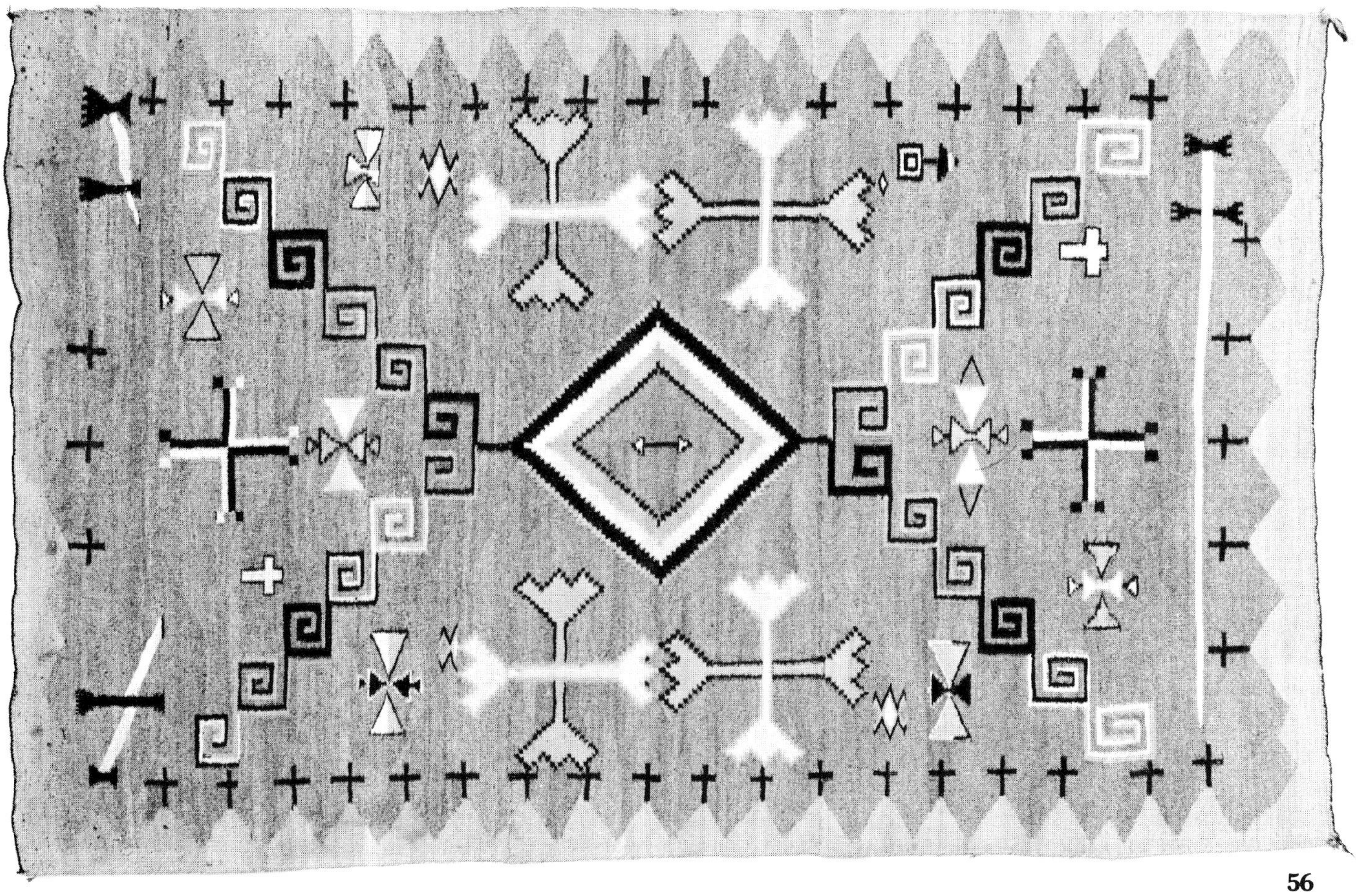

**61 — Crystal Rug**
92 x 54 inches  ca 1903
J. B. Moore's version of a typical Late Classic blanket combining terraced diamonds and diagonal zigzags with stripes in red, black, and white. Published in 1903.

# Western Reservation

The western part has, until recently, been the most remote area of the Navajo Reservation. Many of the design and color usages remain close to those that generally prevailed before 1900. Few regional styles have developed here.

**62 – Coal Mine Mesa Rug**
62 x 32 inches ca 1960s
Storm pattern rug woven in the Coal Mine Mesa "raised outline" technique. Gray, red, and white on a vertically striped ground surrounded by a dark red border.

**63 – Flagstaff Area Rug**
75 x 38 inches ca 1930
Vertically aligned concentric diamonds in a subtle blending in shades of gray, white, and black. The comb serration is typical of the Flagstaff area. Positive-negative border in black and white.

**64 – Single Saddle Blanket**
30 x 30 inches Modern
Vertically aligned diamonds made in diamond stripes derived from Saltillo border designs in white, brown, and tan, on a plain combed gray ground. The intentional mottling of the gray lends a lively accent to the whole saddle blanket.

# Pueblo Weaving

The history of Pueblo weaving goes back into archeological times. About A.D. 800 the Pueblos invented the wide, upright loom, on which they could make wide shawls, blankets, and other garments, from native cotton. When the Spanish arrived in the Southwest, nearly all of the Pueblos were weavers, but today only the Hopi, in northeastern Arizona, continue to weave most traditional Pueblo garments. After the Spanish introduced the sheep, some garments and blankets were woven of wool, but cotton is still the traditional material for most ceremonial garments, made by the Hopis and traded to the other Pueblos. Since about 1880, cotton string has been used for warps, and hand-spun cotton for wefts. Most Hopi garments are woven in plain weave, in which both warp and weft are visible, tapestry being reserved for soft, thick, bed blankets in the Spanish tradition.

**65 — Hopi Maiden Shawl**
38 x 46 inches  Recent
Maiden shawls are traditionally worn by unmarried girls, but others also wear them at times. It is woven in plain diagonal twill, with red and blue bands woven in commercial 4-ply wool in twill weaves.

**66 — Hopi Wedding Dress**
*(not illustrated)*
54 x 70 inches  Recent
This plain white shawl or manta, woven wider than long, is the traditional shape for dresses and blankets. Cotton twine warp and hand-spun cotton weft. The Navajo "Chief" blanket is an adaption of this shape.

**67 — Man's Ceremonial Kilt**
53 x 23 inches  Recent
In some ceremonies, the man wears a white cotton kilt wrapped around his waist. The embroidery, which is probably similar to that noted by the Spanish, falls at the sides. The design is traditional.

**68 — Man's Kachina Sash**
90 x 11 inches, in two pieces  Recent
White cotton sashes with the decorated ends woven in a brocade weave are worn by men during some ceremonies. The design represents the Broad-faced Kachina.

**69 — Rain Belt or Wedding Belt**
*(not illustrated)*
57 x 6 inches  Modern
Woven rain belt. Many such belts are braided. The long fringe represents falling rain while the knobs at the base of the fring represent clouds. Thus the belt depicts fertility in the wedding ceremony or in various dances.

65

67

68

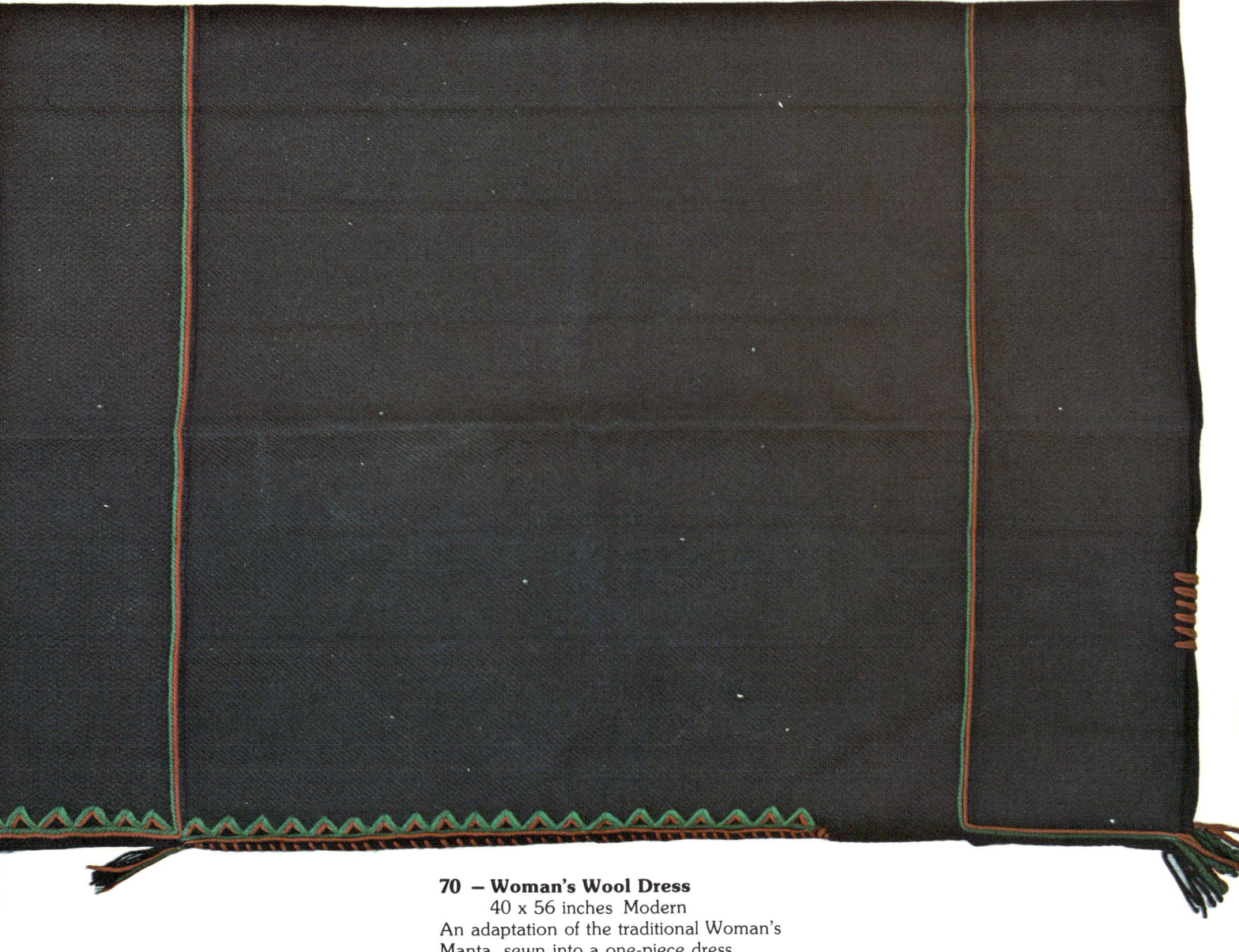

**70 — Woman's Wool Dress**
40 x 56 inches  Modern
An adaptation of the traditional Woman's Manta, sewn into a one-piece dress. Woven from wool, decorated by commercial yarn in red and green.

# Sand-Painting, Yeis, and Yeibechais

According to Navajo religious tradition, none of these tapestries should be woven. Actual sand paintings are altars used in curing ceremonies and are supposed to be destroyed the same day. The first known sand-painting tapestry was woven near Chaco Canyon in 1896. Few were woven until about 1920, when weavers in several areas — Two Gray Hills, Ganado, and Kayenta — began making them.

Yeis are gods in the Navajo pantheon and are depicted in the sand-painting. Rugs with single large Yei figures appear in the Shiprock area about 1910, then more and more complex rugs with rows of Yei figures begin to appear. Yei tapestries from the Shiprock area usually have white or light-colored grounds, those from Greasewood Springs have dark grounds.

Yeibechai rugs depict human dancers wearing Yei masks during ceremonial performances.

**71 — Yei Rug,** Greasewood Springs
*(illustrated on pages 16-17)*
140 x 68 inches ca 1930s
Female Yeis form a colorful row on a black ground enclosed by a simple red border.

**72 — Yei Rug**
*(illustrated on pages 8-9)*
78 x 57 inches ca 1940
A row of female Yei figures on a tan ground and enclosed by multiple-figured borders in the Teec Nos Pos style.

**73 — Yei Pictorial**
61 x 46 inches ca 1940s
A single Yei figure stands in the center of a standard rug of the Rough Rock or Greasewood Springs area.

**74 — Yei,** Shiprock
61 x 35 inches ca 1950s
A row of female Yei figures alternates with a row of stylized corn plants on the tan ground of this finely woven tapestry. The border is typical of the Shiprock area.

**75 76 77 — Gallup Throws**
about 36 x 18 inches Recent
These small, colorful throw blankets, all with variations of Yei figure decoration, are typical of the weaving in the Gallup, New Mexico, area. They have been woven since 1900 for the curio trade, and many exhibit both good weaving and good design.

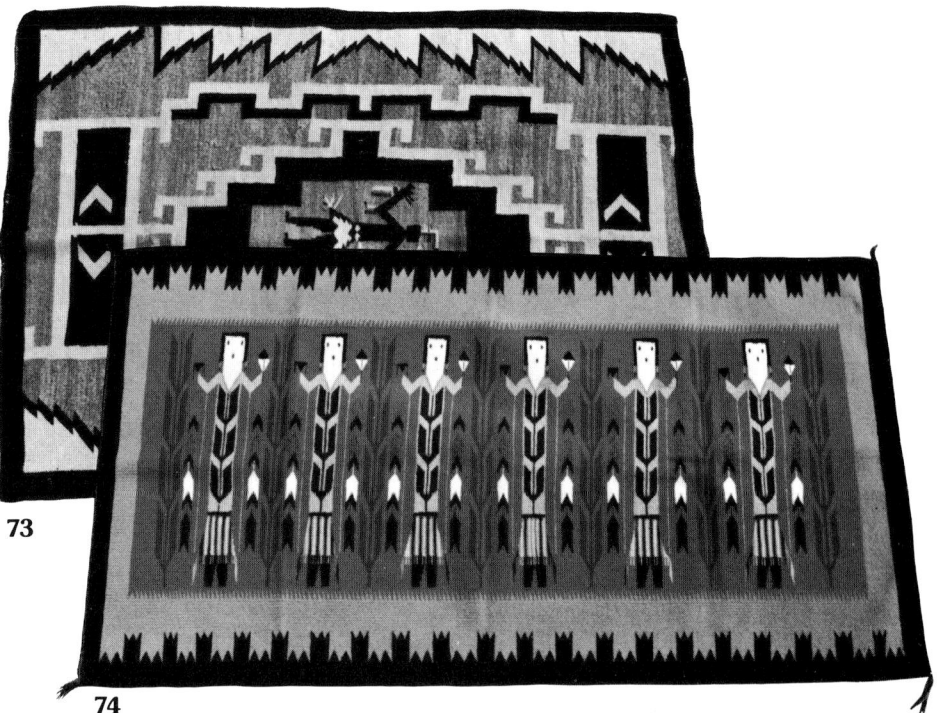

73

74

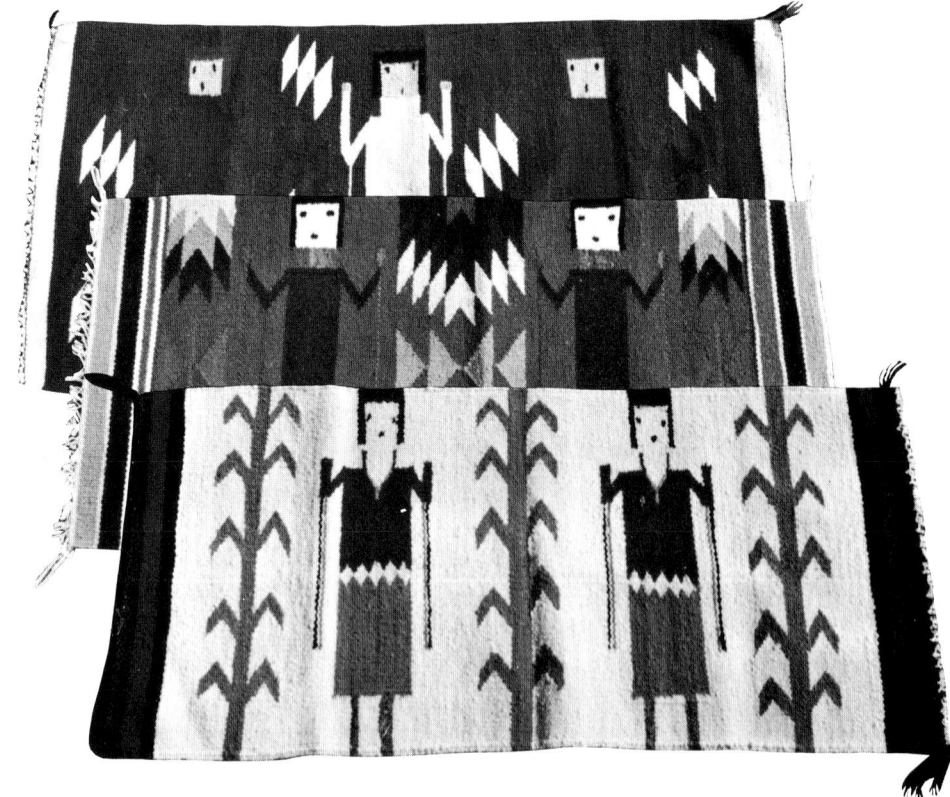

75
76
77

78

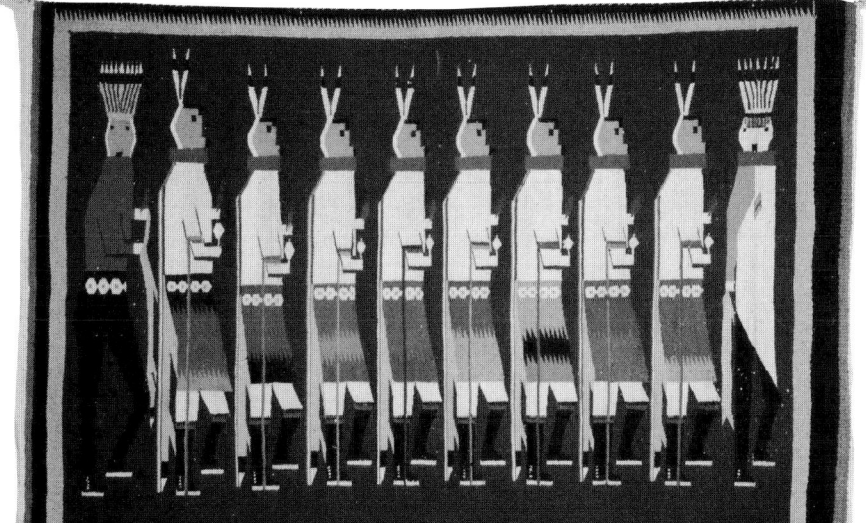

79

**78 — Yeibechai Rug  Greasewood Springs**
68 x 36 inches  ca 1935
Male and female dancers portraying Navajo yeis or gods. The chalk-covered figure is the dance leader.

**79 — Yeibechai Rug  Shiprock**
52 x 35 inches  ca 1960s
Male yei dancers and leader. Profile view is a recent development.

**80 — Yei Rug  Greasewood Springs**
*(not illustrated)*
63 x 44 inches  ca 1960s
Row of female yeis with ceremonial paraphanalia on black ground.

**81 – Sand Painting Tapestry**
48 x 44 inches  ca 1950
A pictorial representation of Mother Earth and Father Sky figures which are used in several ceremonies. The tan ground suggests the fine sand base of real sand paintings.

**82 — Yeibechai Rug**
132 x 89 inches  ca 1940s
Male Yeibechai dancers wearing round-headed masks form a row with the dance leader at the right. Above them, separated by two corn stalks, is a row of female Yeibechai dancers with square masks.

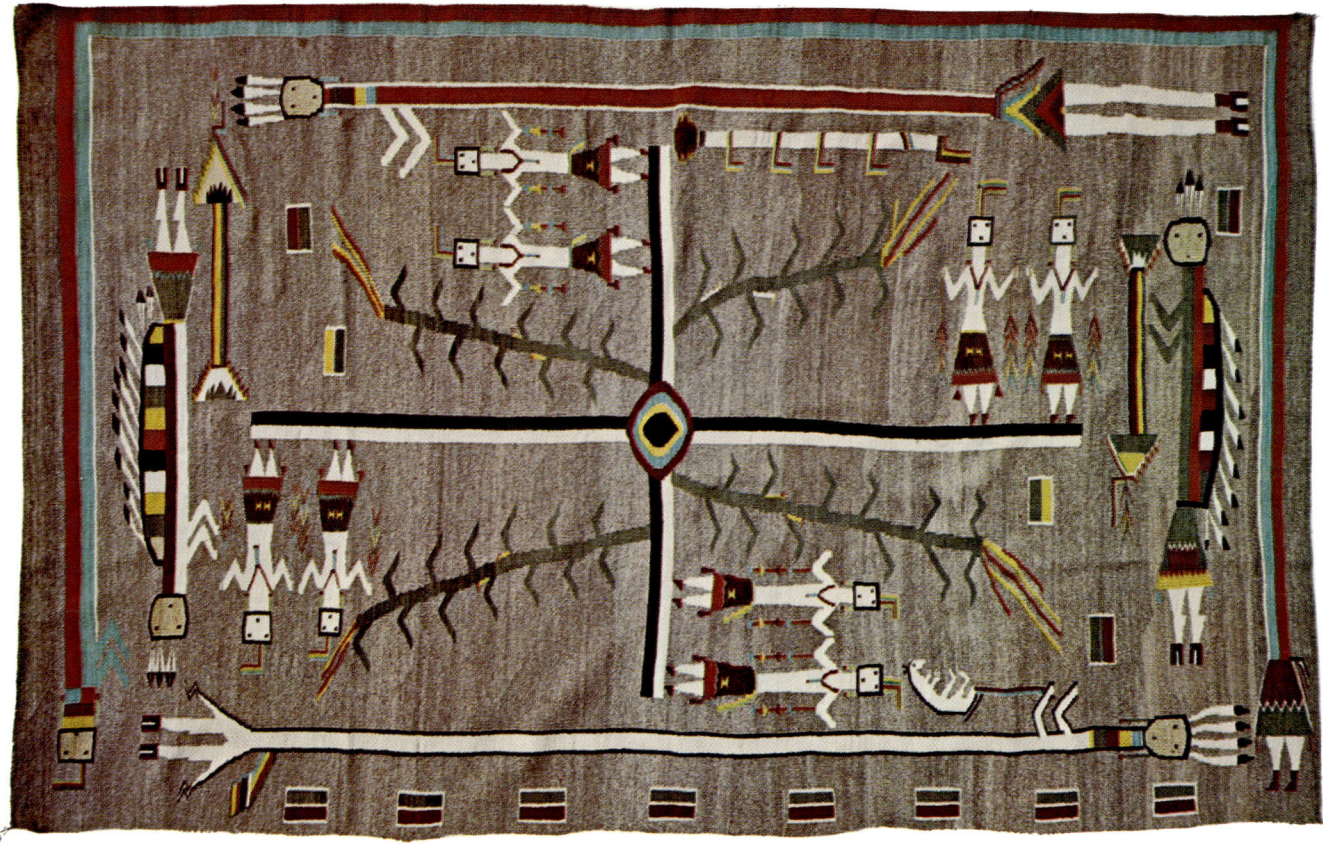

**83 — Kayenta Sand Painting Tapestry**
111 x 69 inches  ca 1925
A pictorial representation of the Whirling Logs sand painting altar of the Night Chant ceremony. The rainbow figure which forms the border should open to the east.

# Teec Nos Pos

Teec Nos Pos, Arizona, is located very near the Four Corners, that is, where Arizona, New Mexico, Colorado, and Utah come together. After 1900, when fine serrate outline style declined elsewhere, the Teec Nos Pos weavers continued to weave it and elaborated on it by adopting some elements of the Crystal-Two Gray Hills patterns and developing some geometric elements of their own. Many colors may be used in the same rug, usually to outline the design elements. Many finely woven rugs came from the Teec Nos Pos region.

**84 — Teec Nos Pos**
89 x 52 inches  ca 1910
In this rug, a bold, massive border in red, black, and gray, which surrounds the central panel of vertically aligned outline serrate diamonds, is relieved by feather motifs and, at the ends, elements taken from sand paintings.

**85 — Teec Nos Pos**
60 x 43 inches  ca 1950
Derived from the early Storm Pattern motif, this striking rug features tan, white, gray, and a touch of red on a black background, an unusual color choice for Navajo weavers. Multiple borders.

**86 — Teec Nos Pos**
60 x 33 inches  ca 1935
Vertically arranged serrate diamonds, each outlined in contrasting colors on a neutral gray ground formed by a bold Greek Fret border in stark black and white.

**87 — Teec Nos Pos Area** *(not illustrated)*
59 x 35 inches  ca 1910
Central motif of serrate outline diamonds surrounded by terraced fret motifs on the sides and at the top. Plain double border. Natural colors with touches of red. Badly faded.

**88 — Northern Reservation Rug**
82 x 57 inches  ca 1930s
Stepped interlocking borders; large, bold, paired, central, terraced-edge diamond motifs, and use of bows and arrows, suggest a northern origin for this well-woven rug.

**89 — Northern Reservation Rug**
76 x 50 inches  ca 1930
Bold, central, stepped-edge diamonds arranged vertically and framed on the sides by interlocking fret borders on a red ground are characteristic of the area north of Chinle, Arizona.

**90 – Teec Nos Pos**
115 x 67 inches  ca 1935-40
Complex geometric pattern of vertically arranged terraced figures surrounded by multiple geometric figures enclosed by two intricately figured borders.

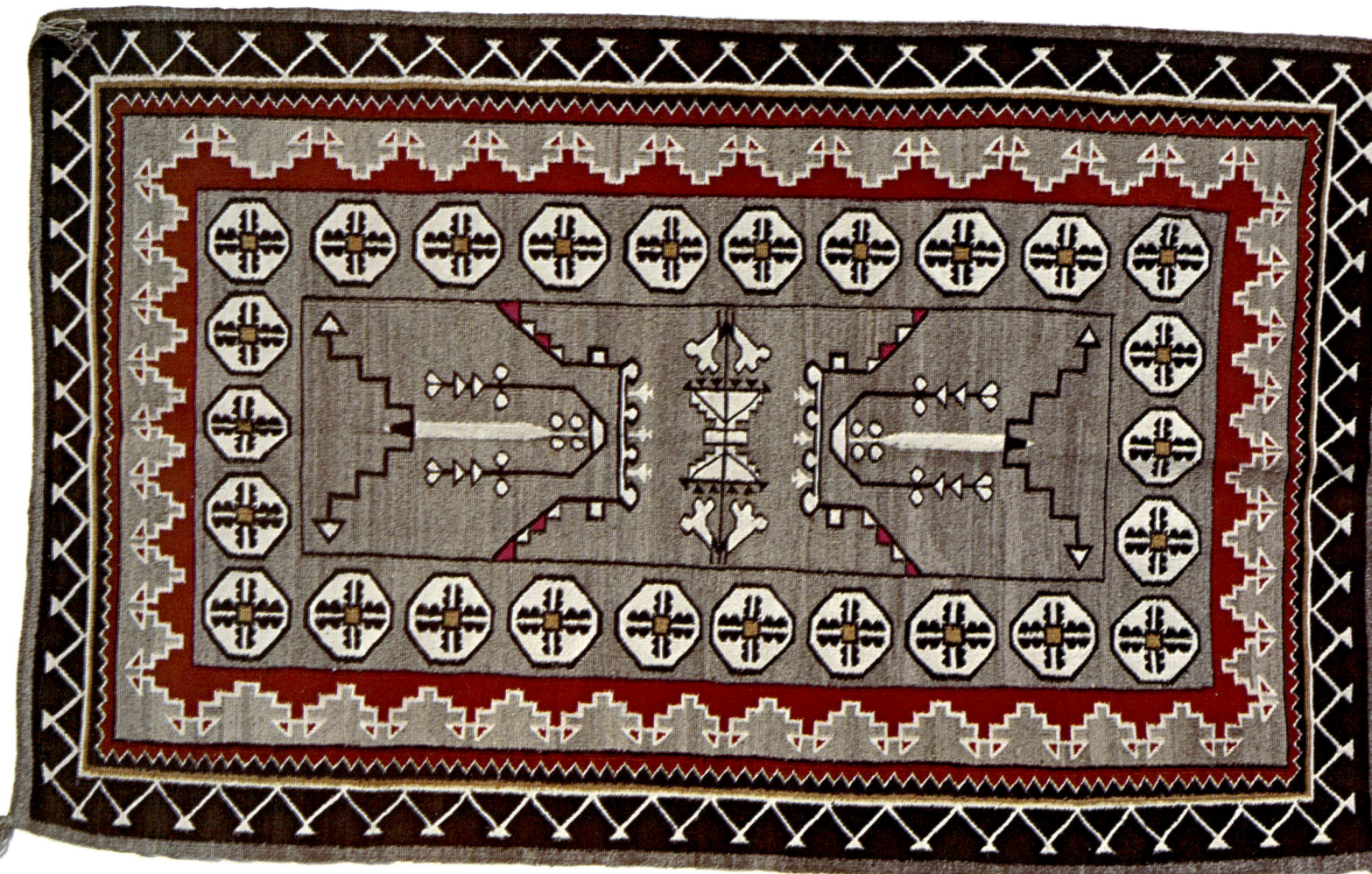

**91 — Teec Nos Pos**
    75 x 47 inches  ca 1935-40
Symmetrical design of linear and semi-naturalistic motifs on neutral gray ground surrounded by five borders of which four are figured in geometric motifs.

# Wide Ruins

In 1938, Bill and Sallie Wagner Lippincott bought Wide Ruins Trading Post south of Ganado. Working with their weavers, they started a revival of early designs and encouraged the return to old native vegetal dyes and the development of new ones. By 1950, the Wide Ruin rug with fine design and subtle vegetal colors in earthy reds, browns, and yellows had all but replaced the standard Navajo rug in red, black, and white in favor, and revival ideas gradually spread out to nearby trading posts such as Pine Springs, Burntwater, and even Klagetoh.

**92 — Wide Ruins Rug**
62 x 43 inches  ca 1960s
Borderless rug in earthy vegetal colors features zoned stripes and panel design made of zigzags done in a derived Saltillo serrate style.

# Navajo Twills

The weaving of heavy twill fabrics began among the Navajo about 1875. Most twills were relatively small and were made for use as saddle blankets, renowned throughout the West. Many of these wound up as throw rugs, and about 1940 the Navajo began weaving larger ones as rugs. They are sometimes known as double-woven rugs. There is no real special area for twills, but many are woven in the western reservation area.

**93 — Twill Double Saddle Blanket**
63 x 29 inches  ca 1960s
A simple all-over design in red and gray, which gives a subtle striped pattern.

**94 – Double Saddle Blanket Twill**
65 x 33 inches  ca 1950
Complex all-over twill pattern with interrupted diamond twill alternating with squares of vertical "beading".

**95 – Double Saddle Blanket Twill**
64 x 31 inches  ca 1960s
Heavy fabric in the interrupted diamond twill pattern, in black, red, and white.

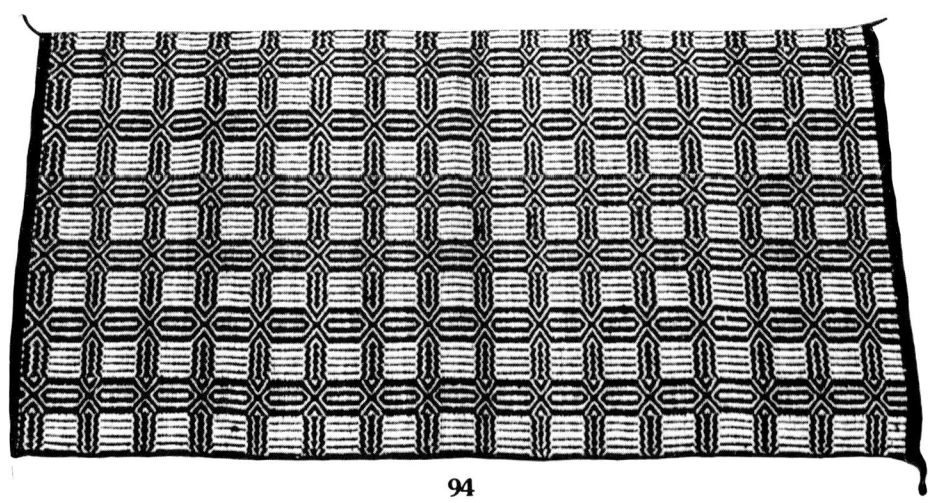

94

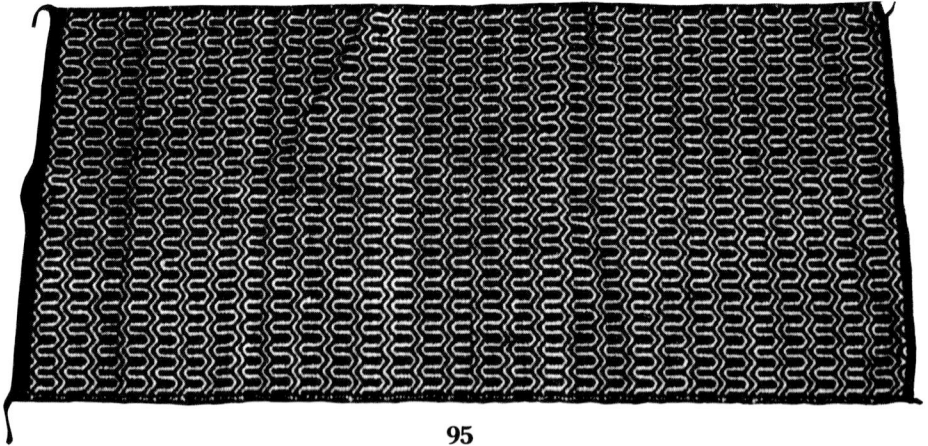

95

# Pictorial Rugs

Blankets and rugs with pictorial designs have been a part of Navajo weaving since the mid-1800s. Early pictorials usually depicted such things as livestock, cornstalks, birds, coffee and flour sacks, can labels, initials, railroad trains, and occasionally humans. Since the 1930s, increasingly full pictorial compositions, including circus animals and landscapes have been woven. One center for pictorial weaving is the Lukachukai Mountains area of northeast Arizona.

### 96 — Pictorial
149 x 104 inches ca 1925
The unusually complex corn and bird motif featured in this large rug is partially pictorial and partly taken from sand painting design. The pictorial content suggests that it was woven in the northern reservation.

### 97 — Lukachukai Area
44 x 36 inches ca 1960s
This small rug pictures a variation of the Great Seal of the United States — the spread eagle clasping arrows in his claws — woven in Navajo tapestry on a golden ground.

### 98 — Cornstalk and Bird Pictorial
*(illustrated on page 68)*
124 x 51 inches ca 1920s
This long, relatively narrow rug has a complex border enclosing the cornstalk and bird motif but interrupted by two cow figures in the 1880s style.

### 99 — Spread Eagle Pictorial Lukachukais
49 x 45 inches ca 1950s
The Spread Eagle motif, from the Great Seal of the United States, was copied by many Indian tribes in various kinds of artifacts. This Navajo tapestry is a wall-hanging.

96

97

99

**100 — Shiprock Area**
 92 x 64 inches ca 1930
An all-over pattern of feathers arranged in vertical rows, red and white or gray and white on a black ground make this a very unusual rug.

**101 — Pictorial**
 52 x 39 inches ca 1950
A standard serrate diamond pattern rug has a small American flag woven into each corner.

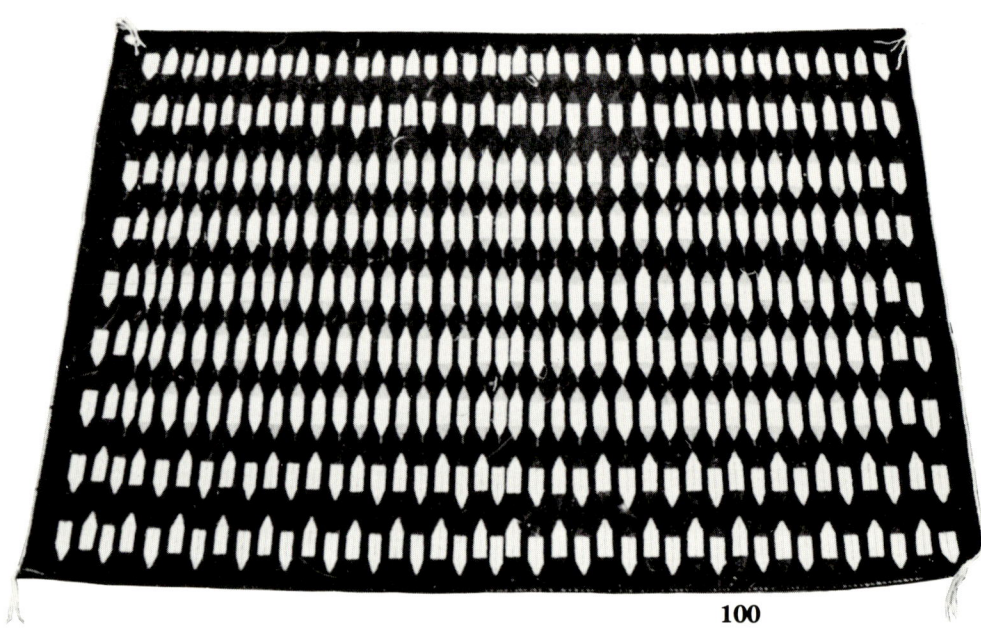

# Novelty Weaves of the Navajo

About 1870, the Navajo weavers developed several novelty weaves. One of these is known as the Two-faced weave, a textile in which each face has a different design, usually a plain one on the back and more complicated figures on the front. Two-faced rugs were never common, and only a few have been woven each year in recent times. Another was the Tufted Weave, called by the Navajo the Fuzzy Weave, because it resembled a sheep pelt. These enjoyed some popularity in the late 1800s and continue to be made today in limited numbers.

### 102 — Two-faced Rug
87 x 55 inches ca 1885

An excellent geometric pattern example of two-face weaving in fine condition. Not a common type weaving, kept production very limited. The dyes are a combination of natural, vegetal and analine. There is no particular area to which they can be attributed.

### 103 — Two-faced Rug
*(not illustrated)*
90 x 58 inches ca 1885

Large Two-faced rug with zoned stripes on the back and a Navajo terraced-edged version of the Saltillo concentric diamond on the front. The aniline colors and fairly coarse yarns are typical of the Two-faced weave.

### 104 — Tufted Saddle Throw
*(not illustrated)*
39 x 24 inches Recent

The saddle throw was used as a pad on the saddle seat, so the soft, fuzzy blanket, tufted with fleeces of angora goat wool was appropriate. The banded design in beading on the rear is typical of the soft weaving of the period.

### 105 — Illusion Rug
72 x 48 inches Recent

Woven in an unusual complex pattern of white, gray and black. The coloration and design caused the perspective to change from different viewing directions.

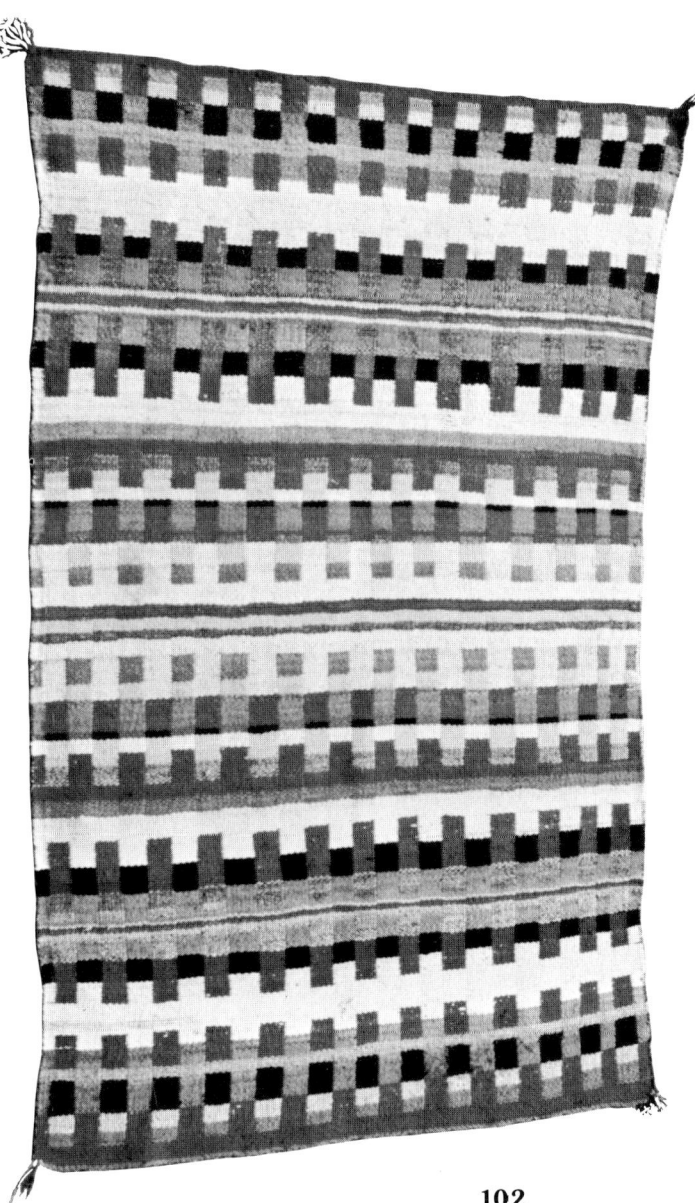

**102**

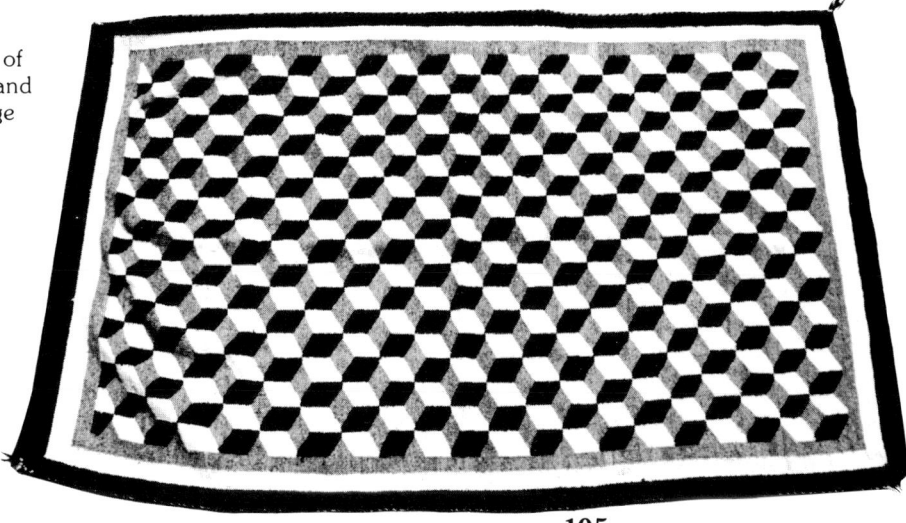

**105**

**98 — Cornstalk and Bird Pictorial**
124 x 51 inches  ca 1920s
This long, relatively narrow rug has a complex border enclosing the cornstalk and bird motif but interrupted by two cow figures in the 1880s style.